California's Favorite Mexican Foods

Presented By

California Home Economics Teachers

Edited By
Gerry Murry Henderson

Graphics By
Robert Knies Design, Inc.

©*Library of Congress Catalog*
Card No. 83-072741
ISBN 0-914159-03-8

©California Cookbook Company
30790 San Pasqual Road, Rancho California, California 92390

CALIFORNIA'S FAVORITE MEXICAN FOODS

I wish I had a dollar for every time my wife has said "Let's go out for some Mexican Food!" It seems that Laura's favorite choice of foods is that of many others in California!

As California has developed its own unique variety of Mexican foods, we asked the California Home Economics Teachers to submit their favorite Mexican recipes.

To these professional teachers whose names and schools appear beneath their recipes, we owe everything for the main content of this book.

To the California Cookbook Company Staff, Doug Herrema, Russ Herrema, Doug Pierce, Bill Horton, and Elaine Lazarus, I say "Thank you for every bit of help you gave!", and further, "How proud I am to be working with professional people like yourselves!"

Robert Knies, of Knies Design, Inc. in Fullerton, did the outstanding artwork throughout the book, and we owe a special thanks to La Victoria Foods, Inc. of Industry, California, who contributed all the photography, including the front cover!

Likewise, the Home Economist at La Victoria Foods, Inc., Marlene Brown contributed all the recipes which identify the color pictures throughout the book. Thank you Marlene!

Few people realize the tedious and time consuming task involved in editing recipes thoroughly, and to Gerry Murry Henderson, of Temple City High School, we owe a big applause for her outstanding job!

Having published these California Home Economics Teachers cookbooks for many years now, we hope that you, as the purchaser, are pleased with the quality and content of the book, as we look forward to publishing others in the years to come.

GRADY W. REED, OWNER
CALIFORNIA COOKBOOK COMPANY

P.S. PLEASE NOTE THE REORDER PAGE IN THE BACK OF THE COOKBOOK!

CALIFORNIA HOME ECONOMICS TEACHERS ADVISORY COMMITTEE

Anderson, Jill
Santa Paula High School, Santa Paula

Benekos, George
Santiago Junior High School, Orange

Black-Eacker, Ellen
Nogales High School, La Puente

Blass, Sue
Valhalla High School, El Cajon

Estes, Marianne
La Mirada High School, La Mirada

Frank, Polly
Lakewood High School, Lakewood

Glennan, Renee
Sequoia Jr. High School, Simi Valley

Henderson, Gerry
Temple City High School, Temple City

Hibma, Grace
Office of Los Angeles County
Superintendent of Schools, Consultant,
Consumer & Homemaking Education

Himenes, Peggy
Actis Junior High School, Bakersfield

Hsieh, Linda
Alhambra High School, Alhambra

Hulen, Donna Lyn
Los Alamitos High School,
Los Alamitos

Lash, Mary
Paramount High School, Paramount

Lundy, Jeri
Grossmont High School, La Mesa

Lopez, Karen
San Luis Obispo High School
San Luis Obispo

Matsuno, Dale
Montebello Intermediate School
Montebello

Mitchell, Eudora
Norwalk High School, Norwalk

Pace, Sally
Woodlake High School, Woodlake

Pendleton, Susie
Cerritos High School, Cerritos

Phipps, Louise
Washington Middle School, Vista

Pereira, Marilyn
Hanford High School, Hanford

Priestley, Roberta
Alhambra High School, Alhambra

Pringle, Adrienne
Valley View Junior High School,
Simi Valley

Rayl, Charla
El Toro High School, El Toro

Richmond, Mary E.
San Luis Obispo High School
San Luis Obispo

Ruth, Lynda
La Mirada High School, La Mirada

Sherrill, Julie
Dos Palos High School, Dos Palos

Shrock, Bonnie
Kearny High School, San Diego

Traw, Marianne
Ball Junior High School, Anaheim

Wildermuth, Ellie
La Canada High School, La Canada

COLOR PHOTOGRAPHY CREDITS

Cover Photograph
**Courtesy of La Victoria Foods, Inc.,
City of Industry, California**

Interior Photographs
Courtesy of La Victoria Foods, Inc.

COLOR PHOTOGRAPHED RECIPES

—CONTENTS—

Special Microwave Feature: All recipes with microwave instructions are marked with the symbol ⓜ.

Notes

Appetizers & Salsas

Party Nachos

1½ lbs. lean ground beef
1 large onion, diced
1 can (30 oz.) refried beans
1 can (7 oz.) green chiles, diced
2 cups jack cheese, grated
2 cups cheddar cheese, grated

1 bottle green chile salsa
½ cup green onions, chopped
1 cup black olives, diced
avocado, sliced or chopped
tortilla chips
1 cup sour cream

Brown the ground beef and onions. Spread refried beans in a 10 x 15 inch ovenproof serving dish. Spread browned meat and onions on top. Sprinkle chiles and cheese over the meat. Drizzle the bottle of green chile salsa over the top. Bake, uncovered, in a 375°F oven for about 25 minutes or until hot. Remove from the oven and top with green onions and olives. Place mounds of avocado and sour cream on top before serving. Serve warm with plenty of tortilla chips.

"This recipe was given to me by Jeannette George, who throws great parties!"

Laurie Owen   **Hoover High School, San Diego**

Fish Appetizer

Serves 10 to 12

2 lbs. partially defrosted halibut or
    other white firm fish or scallops
2 teaspoons lemon rind
1½ cups freshly squeezed
    lemon juice
1 cup onion finely chopped
1 medium tomato, seed, drained
    and chopped

1 can (3 oz.) green chiles, chopped
2 ripe avocados, chopped
2 tablespoons cilantro, chopped
1½ to 2 teaspoons salt
cilantro and tortilla chips,
    for garnish
¼ cup green onion, chopped

Slice fillets at a 45° angle into paper thin pieces; if scallops are used, dice or slice them thinly. Drain fish well. Place in a shallow glass rectangular dish and cover with lemon juice, mixed with lemon peel. Mix fish and lemon juice well with fork. Refrigerate 2 hours. Fish will turn white. Drain off lemon juice and add remaining ingredients. Cover and refrigerate until well chilled. Garnish with cilantro and serve with tortilla chips.

Sharon Turner   **El Dorado High School, Placentia**

Cream Cheese Appetizer

1 block (8 oz.) cream cheese
    (room temperature)
1 jar (8 oz.) chile salsa

¼ cup parsley, chopped
crackers
chips

Place cream cheese block (room temp) on serving platter. Pour chile salsa over the block so it covers the block. Sprinkle with chopped parsley. Serve with chips or crackers.

It may be spread on the crackers with a knife, or broken off with the cracker.

Penny Putnam   **Divisadero Junior High School, Visalia**

Chingalingas Appetizer

Yields 60 pieces

1 chicken	fresh cilantro, chopped
salt	2 tomatoes, diced
1 garlic clove	1 teaspoon chicken bouillon
1 bay leaf	granules
1 teaspoon oil	12 flour tortillas, 6 to 8 inch
1 small onion, minced	cooking oil
1 green bell pepper, diced	guacamole
1 garlic clove, minced	sour cream

Cut up chicken. Place in a large pot. Add water to cover, salt to taste, garlic and bay leaf. Bring to a boil; reduce heat. Cover and simmer 30 minutes. Remove chicken, reserving broth for another use. Let chicken cool and debone. Coarsely shred meat with your fingers. Heat 1 tablespoon oil in a skillet; add onion and bell pepper. Saute for 5 minutes. add garlic, cilantro, tomatoes, bouillon and shredded chicken. Simmer for 15 to 20 minutes to evaporate juices.

Steam flour tortillas, one at a time, to make soft and pliable. Place ½ cup chicken mixture on flour tortillas and roll up, folding in ends like a burrito. Secure with toothpicks. Fry in 1 inch oil in skillet or deep fry until browned. Slice each roll into 5 pieces. Serve with guacamole and sour cream.

Use flour tortillas that are close to home made type. After steaming, they will fold easily and not break.

Maggie Aguirre   **Auburndale Junior High School, Corona**

Jalapeno Quiche

Yields 20 bite-size portions, or 6 to 8 main dish servings

1 can (4 oz.) jalapeno chiles or	6 eggs
1 can (7 oz.) mild green chiles,	salt
seeded and cut in strips	pepper
1¼ pounds cheddar cheese,	dash worchestershire sauce
shredded	

Line bottom of a 10 inch pie plate or 9 inch square baking dish with chile strips. Fill dish with cheese. Pat down. Beat eggs well. Season to taste with salt and pepper and add worcestershire. Pour over cheese. Bake at 375°F for 40 minutes, or until golden and puffed. Cool 15 minutes. Cut into thin wedges or small squares for appetizers or serve as a main dish for luncheon.

Marianne Traw   **Ball Junior High, Anaheim**

L.T.'s Pinwheels

Large flour tortillas (1 ft. size)	garlic salt
chicken, shredded	diced chiles
cream cheese, room temperature	

Combine ingredients and spread the mixture on the large tortillas. Roll them up and wrap them in foil or plastic wrap. Slice when ready to serve.

Anne Dahl   **Ensign Middle School, Newport Beach**

Green Chile Quiche

Yields 60 to 70 bite-size pieces

10 eggs
1 pint cottage cheese
1 teaspoon baking powder
1 teaspoon salt
10 drops tabasco sauce

½ cup flour
1 pound Monterey jack cheese
  snredded
1 can (7 oz.) green chiles, diced
½ cup butter, melted

Preheat oven to 400°F. Butter a 9 x 13 inch glass pan.

In blender, whirl eggs, cottage cheese, baking powder, salt, tabasco sauce and flour. Pour into a large bowl; add cheese, chiles and butter. Mix well. Pour into baking dish and bake for 15 minutes at 400°F. Reduce heat to 350°F and bake 25 to 30 minutes more until set and golden color.

Cut into appetizer size cubes. Serve warm or cold. Keeps 3 to 4 days in refrigerator.

Amber Bradley   *El Capitan High School, Lakeside*

Quesadillas   Ⓜ

Yields 12

1 pound jack cheese, shredded
1 can (7 oz.) California green chiles, chopped
12 corn or flour tortillas
butter, lard, or salad oil for frying (optional)

Mix shredded cheese and green chopped chiles. Divide into 12 equal parts. Place 1/12 of cheese mixture in the center of a tortilla. Fold tortilla over cheese mixture and pin shut with a small wooden skewer. Fry in shallow hot butter, lard or salad oil until crisp, turning occasionally. Drain on paper towels. May be just heated on each side on a medium hot ungreased griddle or frying pan, until the cheese has melted. May also be placed in the microwave oven to melt cheese.

Eudora Mitchell   *Norwalk High School, Norwalk*

Mexi-Skins

Serves 16

8 large potatoes, baked and halved
1½ cups each cheddar cheese and
  Monterey Jack cheese, shredded
½ cup tomatoes, diced
½ cup ripe olives, sliced

½ cup La Victoria Nacho
  Sliced Jalapenos
½ cup green onion, thinly sliced
1 cup guacamole
1 cup any favorite La Victoria Salsa

Step one: Scoop centers from potatoes, leaving ¼ inch thick shells. (Use scooped-out potato for mashed potatoes another time.)

Step two: Fill shells equally with cheeses, tomato, olives, Jalapenos, and green onion.

Step three: Bake in a 450° oven for 5 minutes, or just till heated through. Serve with guacamole and Salsa.

La Victoria Foods, Inc.   *City of Industry, CA*

Tortizzas

Serves 6

2 to 3 slices bacon
1 drop tabasco sauce
½ teaspoon garlic salt
1 cup refried beans

3 tortillas or English muffins
(cut in half)
2 tablespoons green onion, chopped
1 cup cheddar cheese, grated

Fry bacon in skillet until crisp. Drain bacon on paper towel and crumble. Mix tabasco sauce and garlic salt into refried beans. Spread bean mixture on tortilla halves or English muffin halves. Top with chopped onion, then grated cheese. Plaze tortizzas on broiler pan. Broil five to eight minutes or until cheese is bubbly. Garnish with crumbled bacon on top.

Tortizzas are an excellent appetizer or open-faced sandwich to serve with a nice bowl of soup. Add a glass of milk and a fruit for a well-balanced meal.

Joanne Fial   **East Middle School, Downey**

Green Chile Cheese Appetizer

Serves 10 to 12

1 can (7 oz.) green chiles, diced
1½ cups sharp cheddar cheese,
grated
2½ cups jack cheese, grated

1 tablespoon flour
2 eggs, beaten
2 tablespoons milk

Mix together the green chiles, the cheeses and the flour. Beat eggs and stir in milk. Add the eggs and milk to the green chile and cheese mixture and mix well.

Put into a greased 9 x 12 inch Pyrex dish. Bake at 375°F for 30 minutes. Cut into squares and serve.

Roberta Forbes   **Marshall Junior High School, Long Beach**

Tortilla Cheese Rolls

Yields approximately 24 appetizers

1 jar (5 oz.) processed cheese spread with jalapenos
1½ cup (6 oz.) jack cheese, shredded
4 (8 inch) flour tortillas
1 can (4 oz.) green chiles, drained and diced
1 jar (4 oz.) pimientos, drained well and sliced

Combine cheeses in bowl or food processor. Spread one tortilla evenly with ¼ of cheese mixture to within ½ inch border of tortilla. Top with second tortilla, then spread with ¼ more cheese mixture and sprinkle with ½ of the green chiles and pimentos. roll tortillas as tightly as possible, being careful not to let top tortilla slide forward. Finished roll should be about 2 inches in diameter. Wrap tightly in foil.

Make second roll using remaining ingredients. Place wrapped rolls in refrigerator and chill at least 3 hours or overnight. Remove foil and slice rolls into ¼ inch thick round. Place on greased baking sheets and bake in a 375°F oven for 15 to 20 minutes, or until lightly crisp on top.

Karen Bennett   **Valencia High School, Placentia**

Panchitos

Serves 12 or more

2 pkgs. Crescent Rolls (15 oz.)
1 can (7 oz.) chili con carne
½ cup cheddar cheese, grated

2 whole green chiles,
    cleaned and chopped fine
¼ teaspoon garlic powder

Press crescent rolls together on a large breadboard. make them into a large rectangle. Cut into 2½ inch squares. Mix chili con carne, cheese and green chiles into a medium mixing bowl. Stir in garlic powder. Place about 1 teaspoon of mixture in center of square and fold each corner to the center and pinch together. Place each panchito onto a cookie sheet and bake approximately 10 minutes at 450°F, until golden brown. Serve on a platter with a bowl of salsa in the middle.

I like this recipe because it's easy to make and tastes yummy! Make them in the morning — cover, bake later and serve hot. Makes a wonderful one period cooking day. Ole!.

Tess Osborne   *Columbus Tustin Intermediate School, Tustin*

Mock Empanadas

Yields approximately 4 dozen

1 lb. lean ground beef
1 envelope onion red pepper
pinch ground red pepper

1 cup (4 oz.) cheddar cheese, grated
3 packages (8 oz.) refrigerated
    crescent rolls

Combine first 3 ingredients in a 10 inch skillet and brown. Drain fat. Add cheese and stir until melted. Remove from heat. Separate dough into triangles and cut each in half. Spoon about 1 tablespoon meat mixture onto each triangle. Fold edges into center and seal well. Bake on ungreased cookie sheet about 15 minutes or until golden.

Great for parties!

Jan Oliver   *Irvine High School, Irvine*

Chili Puff

Servies 12

1 can Pillsbury biscuits (10)
1 can (17 oz.) chili con carne
1 whole green chile, cleaned and
    chopped fine

¼ teaspoon salt
⅛ teaspoon pepper
⅛ teaspoon garlic powder
½ cup Monterey jack cheese,
    grated

Cut biscuits into ⅓ pieces. Mix chili con carne, green chile, salt, pepper and garlic powder. Place ⅓ biscuit piece of biscuit into a miniature muffin tin and press down. (Spray with Pam first.) Press into biscuit a small amount of mixture. Bake in oven at 450°F for 10 minutes, or a little longer. Sprinkle jack cheese over each puff and bake another 2 minutes, or until cheese melts.

Add a chili puff to your Cinco de Mayo party. They are a one bite snack and disappear quickly.

Tess Osborne   *Columbus Tustin Intermediate School, Tustin*

Stuffed Cheese Roll

8 oz. Velveeta cheese with
  jalapeno, room temperature
1 can (16 oz.) refried beans
1 can (7 oz.) green chiles,
  chopped

olives
2 to 3 green onions, chopped
hot picante sauce or salsa
lettuce
assorted crackers or chips

Roll out room temperature cheese between 2 sheets of waxed paper to approximately 10 x 13 inch rectangle. Remove top sheet of waxed paper. Spread a layer of beans, then green chiles, olives and green onion. If serving soon, top with desired amount of picante sauce or salsa. Omit some of the juice. Roll up into a log, chill or place on lettuce and garnish. Serve with assorted crackers or chips and a serving knife.

If made ahead, omit picante sauce and pour over top of cheese log as part of your garnish. Make as hot or mild as you wish. Other options are layer of cream cheese or chopped pimento.

Maggie Aguirre   **Aburndale Junior High School, Corona**

Chili Cheese Puffs

Yields 48 pieces

1 package (17¼ oz.) frozen
  puff pastry, thawed
12 oz. cheddar cheese, shredded

4 teaspoons chili powder
salt to taste
1 egg, slightly beaten

Roll both sheets of puff pastry into two 12 x 16 inch rectangles. Toss cheese and chili powder together. Sprinkle half the cheese mixture on each rectangle of puff pastry. Salt to taste.

Starting on long edges, roll opposite edges to center. Brush with beaten egg. Chill rolls 1 hour. Slice into ½ inch slices. Place on greased cookie sheet and bake at 425°F for 15 minutes.

Yummy!

Sharon Kleven   **San Gabriel High School, San Gabriel**

Dee's Cheese Log

Serves "A Group of Snackers"

3 to 4 drops tabasco sauce
8 oz. cream cheese, softened
pinch seasoned salt (or to taste)
small jar shoestring pimento

small can chiles, diced
small can black olives, chopped
middle size box Velveeta cheese,
  softened

Add 3 to 4 drops tabasco to the soft cream cheese. Add pinch of seasoned salt and cream. Drain and chop pimento and chiles and fold into cream cheese. Drain olives and carefully fold into cream cheese mixture.

Roll out softened Velveeta cheese between sheets of waxed paper to a rectangle about 8 x 11 inches and 1/4 inch thick. Place cream cheese mixture in center of rectangle. Fold long ends and pinch together. Flop over with seam on bottom; pinch ends together. Can refrigerate until serving time. Serve surrounded by crackers.

Judy Cornwall   **Poly High School, Long Beach**

Mexican Gorditas

Serves 8

3 cups Masa Harina
2 cups water, warm
1/2 teaspoon salt
1/2 pound jack cheese or cheddar,
   shredded
2 ripe avocados

2 medium tomatoes
4 tablespoons sour cream
few grains of salt
few grains of pepper
dash of paprika

Mix 3 cups of Masa Harina with a little of the warm water gradually until the two cups have been added. Sprinkle the salt and knead. Divide into 8 parts and press into round cakes of about two inch diameter. Pre-heat a griddle (lightly greased) or a frying pan (lightly greased) over a medium flame or element. Fry slowly for about three minutes on each side or until lightly brown. Place cakes on a platter and sprinkle with grated cheese. Place a small slice of avocado and a small sliced wedge of tomato on top. Add sour cream in the center, and salt and pepper to tast and a dash of paprika.

Refried beans can be spread on the cakes before grated cheese is added. These are popular in Sonora, Mexico.

Elda G. Benson   **Corona Junior High School, Corona**

Super Nachos   Ⓜ

Serves 4

1 16 oz. package tortilla chips
1 1/2 cups each cheddar cheese and
   Monterey Jack cheese, shredded
1 cup La Victoria Salsa Suprema

1/2 cup La Victoria Nacho
   Sliced Jalapenos
1/2 cup tomatoes, diced
1/4 cup ripe olives, sliced

Garnishes: La Victoria Salsa Suprema, sour cream, sliced onion, guacamole

Spread chips out on an ovenproof platter. Sprinkle with cheeses. Microwave 1 to 2 minutes, or heat in a 350°F. oven till cheese melts.

Spoon on the 1 cup Salsa; top with remaining ingredients. Garnish as desired.

La Victoria Foods, Inc.   **City of Industry, CA**

Hot Bean Dip

8 oz. cream cheese, softened
1 large can Frito Bean Dip
20 drops tabasco sauce
dash of salt
4 oz. jack cheese, grated

4 oz. sharp cheddar cheese,
   grated
1 small carton sour cream
1 package Lawry's Enchilada Mix
1/2 cup green onions, chopped

Mix all ingredients together, except a small amount of the cheddar. Put into a casserole or baking dish. Top with the reserved cheddar. Bake for 15 to 20 minutes at 350°F. Serve with tortilla chips.

This is one everyone raves about!

Julie Hampton   **Franklin Junior High School, Long Beach**

Green Chile Cheese Puffs

Yields about 2½ dozen

½ cup soft butter
2 cups cheddar cheese, grated
½ teaspoon dry mustard
½ teaspoon salt
2 teaspoons canned green chiles,
    finely chopped

2 teaspoons pimento,
    finely chopped
½ teaspoon Worcestershire sauce
1¼ cup sifted all purpose flour

Beat butter, cheese, mustard, salt, chiles, pimentos and Worcestershire sauce together until well blended. Add flour and mix to a stiff dough. Roll level tablespoons of dough into small balls. Place on ungreased baking sheet. Press down lightly with tines of fork. Bake in oven at 350°F for about 15 minutes.

Serve warm or cold.

Nan Paul   *Grant Middle School, Escondido*

Sombrero Spread

½ lb. lean ground beef
½ cup onions, chopped
¼ cup extra hot catsup
1½ teaspoons chili powder
½ teaspoon salt

1 can red kidney beans,
    with liquid
¼ cup stuffed olives, sliced
¼ cup onions, chopped
¼ cup sharp cheese, shredded

Brown beef and onions. Add catsup, chili powder, and salt. Mash in kidney beans and heat through. Garnish with stuffed olives, onions, and cheese. Serve with warm corn chips.

Yvonne Lindrum   *Schurr High School, Montebello*

Chalupa Dip

Serves 12 to 18

1½ pounds ground beef
1 cup onion, chopped
1½ teaspoons salt
pepper
1 teaspoon chili powder
¼ teaspoon garlic powder
pinch crushed chile pepper,
    (red, dried)
1 large can refried beans

4 oz. can green chiles, diced
3 cups cheddar cheese, shredded
7 ounce can green chile salsa
1½ bunches green onions, chopped
4½ ounces ripe olives, chopped
2 cups guacamole
8 ounces sour cream
2 tomatoes, chopped

In a large skillet, brown the meat, onion, salt, pepper, chili powder, garlic powder, and chile pepper. Stir in refried beans and diced green chiles. Pour into an ovenproof casserole. Sprinkle on cheese and pour over the green chile salsa. Top with chopped green onions. This may now be covered and refrigerated until ready to bake and serve.

Bake at 400°F for 30 to 45 minutes, depending on whether it was refrigerated or not. Garnish with olives, chopped tomatoes, guacamole and sour cream. Serve with tortilla chips.

Jennifer Gierman   *Ball Junior High School, Anaheim*

Frijole Dip

¾ cup dried pinto beans
2½ cups hot water
½ teaspoon salt
juice of ½ lemon
1 teaspoon Worcestershire sauce
1 tablespoon mayonnaise

1 clove garlic, minced
1/8 teaspoon salt
1/4 teaspoon hot pepper sauce
4 green onions, chopped
1 package tortilla chips

Soak beans in water and ½ teaspoon salt overnight. (Or combine with water; bring to a boil and cook for 2 minutes. Remove from heat and let stand 1 hour.) Cook until tender, about 2 hours. Drain. Place in blender the beans, lemon juice, worcestershire sauce, mayonnaise, minced garlic, salt, hot pepper sauce, 2 chopped green onions and blend until smooth. Place in a serving dish and garnish with remaining chopped onions. Serve with tortilla chips.

Antoinette De Neve   *Jones Jr. High School, Baldwin Park*

"Hearty" Bean Dip   Ⓜ

Serves 4 for Supper or an appetizer for a group

1½ pounds ground turkey
1 medium avocado
1 medium tomato
1 small can olives, sliced
1 can vegetarian refried beans

⅓ cup salsa
2 cups natural cheddar cheese,
  grated
1 cup Nice'n Light sour cream
no salt tortilla chips

Place ground turkey in center of glass baking dish, (it may still be frozen). Put in microwave under FULL POWER for 5 minutes at a time. Remove, drain, chop and repeat until all ground turkey is cooked.

While turkey is cooking, chop avocado, tomato, drain olives. Mix these together and set aside.

To turkey, add refried beans and salsa. Sprinkle grated cheese on top and return to microwave for 2½ minutes. Spread sour cream over mixture. Top with mixed avocado, tomatoes and olives. Serve hot with tortilla chips.

This recipe is for a healthier heart!

Mary Cronkhite   *Antelope Valley High School, Lancaster*

Chile Con Queso   Ⓜ

Yields about 3½ cups

1 pound pasturized processed cheese spread, cut into 1 inch cubes
1 can (10¾ oz.) condensed cream of mushroom soup
1 can (4 oz.) green chilies, drained and chopped
1/8 teaspoon garlic powder
jalapeno pepper, sliced (optional)

In a 1½ quart casserole, combine all ingredients, except jalapeno pepper. Mix well. Microwave on MEDIUM HIGH for 8 to 10 minutes, or until mixture can be stirred smooth, stirring every 2 minutes. Garnish with jalapeno pepper if desired. Serve hot with tortillas or corn chips.

Pat Fiscus   *Sinaloa Junior High, Simi Valley*

Jeane Whitney's Hot Bean Soup Ⓜ

Yield 3 cups

1 can (#2½) pork and beans in
   tomato sauce (3½ cups)
½ cup sharp cheese, grated
1 teaspoon chili powder
½ teaspoon garlic powder
½ teaspoon seasoned salt

dash cayenne pepper
2 teaspoons vinegar
2 teaspoons worcestershire sauce
½ teaspoon liquid smoke
4 slices crisp cooked bacon
tortilla chips for dipping

Mash beans with potato masher or whirl in blender. Stir in rest of ingredients, except bacon. Mix well. Heat slowly in the top of a double boiler or in microwave oven at 50% power until hot. Sprinkle crumbled bacon on top and serve hot with tortilla chips for dipping.

Special recipe submitted in memory of a dear friend and long time school secretary at San Luis Obispo High School.

Mary E. Richmond   *San Luis Obispo High School, San Luis Obispo*

Chile Con Queso

Serves 6 to 8

1 can (15 oz.) stewed tomatoes
1 can (4 oz.) chiles, diced
1 small onion, chopped
1 pound cheddar cheese, shredded

1 pound Mexican Velveeta,
   hot or mild to suit taste
tortilla chips or vegetables
   for dipping

Pour tomatoes and diced chiles into electric fondue pot or chafing dish. Add chopped onion and shredded cheddar cheese. Cut Mexican Velveeta into chunks and add to mixture. Stir mixture and allow to melt, stirring occasionally. Serve with tortilla chips or vegetables for dipping, such as jicama strips, celery or carrot sticks, etc.

Connie Kensinger   *El Camino Junior High School, Santa Maria*

Spunky Chile-Cheese Dip

Serves 8 to 10

1 loaf round sourdough bread, unsliced
12 oz. cheddar cheese, shredded
12 oz. Monterey jack cheese, shredded
1 jar (12 oz.) green chile salsa
1 can (4 oz.) green chiles, diced
tortilla chips

Slice and top off bread and save for lid. Hollow out bread leaving ½ inch shell all around. (Save bread cubes for dipping.)

Layer half the cheeses, half the salsa and half the chiles in hollow bread shell. Repeat layers. Put bread lid on top of loaf, wrap in foil and place on cookie sheet. Bake at 350°F for 2 hours. Serve hot dip with tortilla chips or reserved bread cubes.

Penny Niadna   *Golden West High School, Visalia*

Chile Con Queso Dip

Serves 4 to 8

1 pound Velveeta or processed cheese
⅓ cup milk
1 jar (8 oz.) salsa

Cut processed cheese into cubes. Add ⅓ cup milk to a saucepan, over medium heat. Add cheese to saucepan and stir with a wooden spoon until melted. Add salsa to cheese mixture and stir until hot. Keep cheese mixture warm by placing in a fondue pot or the saucepan over sterno or other heat source. Dip chips and enjoy!

This is a very quick and easy delicious dip. Any leftovers are great in an omelette.

Donna Adams Small   **Santana High School, Santee**

Tostada Appetizer   Ⓜ

Serves 10 to 15

1 pound hamburger
1 package taco seasoning
large flour tortillas
1 large can refried beans
1 to 2 tomatoes, diced
1 small can green chiles, diced

1 small can olives, diced
3 to 4 green onions, chopped
1 cup cheddar cheese, grated
1 cup jack cheese, grated
1 cup sour cream
1 cup salsa

Brown the ground beef, drain fat and add taco seasoning. Simmer 5 minutes. Use a 12 inch glass platter and put on tortilla and start adding ingredients listed above in order. Add more or less of each ingredient to your liking. Microwave on HIGH 1 to 2 minutes or until heated through.

Pam Reed   **Redondo Union High School, Redondo Beach**

7 Layer Dip

Serves 4

One: 1 can (16 oz.) refried beans
          2 tablespoons mayonnaise

Two: ¼ cup mayonnaise
          8 oz. sour cream
          ½ package taco seasoning mix

Three: 2 large avocados, mashed
          3 tablespoons mayonnaise with a dash of salt and pepper

Four: ¼ cup each cheddar and mozzarella cheese, finely grated

Five: small can olives, sliced

Six: 1½ large tomatoes, diced

Seven: mild Ortega sauce

Layer everything in order given. Heat or eat cold. Eat with large dip corn chips.

The best.

Vicki Taylor   **Silver Valley High School, Yermo**

Green Chile Sour Cream Dip

Serves 8 to 10

3 cups sour cream
1 medium can green chiles, diced
1/2 cup taco sauce

1 1/2 cups cheddar cheese, grated
salt and pepper to taste

Mix sour cream in a bowl. Add in diced green chiles and taco sauce (medium or hot depending on desired taste). Grate cheese and add to above mixture. Salt and pepper to taste. Refrigerate several hours before serving to enhance flavor. Remove and let stand at room temperature about 20 to 30 minutes before serving.

Using a mild or hot spicy taco sauce certainly changes flavor of this appetizer.

Myrna Orr   **McFadden Intermediate, Santa Ana**

Baja Dip

Serves 8 to 12

1/4 cup cottage cheese
2 tomatoes, chopped
1 bunch green onions, sliced
1 can (4 oz.) Ortega green chiles,
    diced
1/2 cup black olives, sliced

4 dashes tabasco
3 dashes worcestershire
4 tablespoons red wine vinegar
tortilla chips and/or
    cut raw vegetables

Combine all ingredients except chips and vegetables. Cover and refrigerate 2 hours or overnight. Place chips and/or vegetables on platter; serve dip in a bowl.

This dip is much better tasting than it sounds (or looks!). We serve it with crunchy raw vegetables in the summertime.

George Yackey   **Santana High School, Santee**

Dip Delight   Ⓜ

Serves 6 to 8

1/2 pound sharp cheddar cheese
1 jar or can green or red chile dip
    or salsa

1/2 teaspoon hot sauce
1 package tortilla chips

Grate cheese and add to salsa. Add hot sauce and mix. Serve in a bowl for dipping.

Optional: Can be heated in microwave to melt cheese (1 to 3 minutes). Eat cold or warm.

Milly Walls   **El Dorado High School, Placentia**

Marsha's Easy Chili Dip

2 cans chili with beans
2 package (8 oz.) cream cheese

medium to hot red chile salsa,
    to taste

Heat cans of chili and package of cream cheese and stir until the cream cheese melts. Add salsa to taste. Serve with raw vegetables or chips.

Glenell Fuller   **Glendora High School, Glendora**

Layered Taco Dip

1 can (16 oz.) refried beans
1/2 teaspoon chili powder
2 avocados, peeled and mashed
1/2 cup salad dressing
3 strips bacon, fried and cut up
1/4 cup onion, chopped

1/2 teaspoon salt
1 cup ripe olives, chopped
1 cup tomatoes, chopped
1 can (4 oz.) green chiles,
  drained and chopped
1 cup monterey jack cheese,
  shredded

Combine refried beans and chili powder in one bowl. Combine avocado, salad dressing, bacon, onion and salt. Mix well. Layer bean mixture, avocado mixture, then top with layer of olives, tomatoes, green chiles, and top with a layer of cheese. Use a shallow pan. Serve with taco chips.

Barbara Bressler   *Buena Park High School, Buena Park*

Mexicali Cheese Fondue

Serves 6 to 8

1 pound Velveeta cheese, cubed
1 can (1 lb.) whole tomatoes,
  drained and chopped

1 can (4 oz.) Ortega chiles, diced
1 tablespoon onion, chopped
1 package tortilla chips

Put all ingredients except chips together into top of a double boiler. Heat until cheese is melted. Pour into fondue dish or other dish. Serve with tortilla chips.

Shelley Menser   *Palmdale High School, Palmdale*

Ortega Chile Cheese Dip   Ⓜ

Serves 6 to 8

1 can (4 oz.) green chiles, diced
1 pound Velveeta cheese, cubed
1 pound whole tomatoes, well drained, chopped
1 tablespoon onion, minced

Combine all ingredients. Place in a microwave casserole dish and heat for 3 to 5 minutes. Stir after 2 minutes.

Serve this with tortilla strips or Fritos. This recipe was given to me by a 7th grade food student, Michael Taylor.

Marianne Traw   *Ball Junior High School, Anaheim*

Quick Mexican Dip

Serves: 4

1 can (15 oz.) chili without beans
3/4 cup sour cream
1 tablespoon chili powder

1 cup cheddar cheese, grated
1 large package tortilla chips

Heat chili, sour cream and chili powder until hot. Top with grated cheese. Serve with tortilla chips.

Rita Kramer   *Montebello High School, Montebello*

Chili Cheese Dip

Serves 10 to 12

1 can chili beef soup
1 can cheddar cheese soup
1 can green chiles, diced

1 cup cheddar cheese, grated
Tortilla chips or corn chips for
serving

Mix the chili beef soup, cheddar cheese soup and diced green chiles together. Put mixture into a one quart casserole dish and top with grated cheese. Bake at 350°F for 15 to 20 minutes, or until hot and bubbly. Serve with tortilla chips or corn chips.

A great filling for burritos.

Joanne Fial   **East Middle School, Downey**

Avocado Dip

Serves 4

2 avocados
1 tablespoon green onion, chopped
1 tablespoon lemon juice
dash salt

¼ teaspoon chili powder
sprinkle of tabasco sauce
⅓ cup mayonnaise

Mash and mix first six ingredients. Spread mayonnaise on top and refrigerate. When ready to serve, stir in mayonnaise.

Janet Worland   **Silver Valley High School, Yermo**

Frozen Avocado Dip

Yields 3 cups

4 medium avocados
1 package (8 oz.) cream cheese
   at room temperature
2 tablespoons fresh lemon juice

1 tablespoon vinegar
1 tablespoon onion, grated
salt to taste
2 shakes tabasco

Mash avocado. Put in blender along with other ingredients. Blend. Freeze in airtight container. Thaw just before serving. May add chopped tomato, cilantro, ripe olives, if desired.

Good way to use ripe avocados! Of course, you may serve immediately after preparing if desired.

Sharon Kleven   **San Gabriel High School, San Gabriel**

Guacamole

Serves 6 to 8

1 envelope unflavored gelatine
1 cup cold water
½ cup bottled Italian dressing
2 medium ripe avocados

½ cup sour cream
1 tablespoon green onion, chopped
dash hot pepper sauce

Dissolve gelatine in cold water. Add gelatine and all remaining ingredients to blender jar. Blend until smooth, refrigerate until set. Keep refrigerated.

Carolyn Yeutter   **Norco Junior High School, Norco**

Mexican Shrimp Dip ⓜ

Yields 2 cups or serves 6 to 8 people

1 package (8 oz.) cream cheese
1 cup small cooked shrimp
1 can (10 oz.) green chile salsa
1 teaspoon worcestershire sauce

½ teaspoon garlic salt
1 tablespoon 'hot' taco sauce
paprika — to garnish

Mix all ingredients together in a small ovenproof dish. Garnish with a sprinkle of paprika. Bake at 350°F for about 15 minutes or until heated through. Serve **"HOT"** with taco chips.

The microwave can be used for reheating.

A "hot" well-blended flavor makes this dip a good way to start any get-together.

Shirley Blough   **Hillside Junior High School, Simi Valley**

7 Layer Guacamole Dip

Serves 12 to 14

1 can Laura Scudder's jalapeno bean dip
guacamole
½ pint sour cream mixed with ¼ to ½ package of taco seasoning mix
2 to 4 green onions, diced
1 small can ripe olives, sliced
2 tomatoes, diced
cheddar cheese, shredded
jack cheese, shredded

Layer in glass pie or quiche dish as follows: bean dip, guacamole, sour cream, diced onions, olives and tomatoes. Completely cover dip with lots of cheese, more cheddar than jack. Serve with tortilla chips.

The guacamole can be the secret to this dip. Make it fairly spicy with lots of garlic and onion salt.

Mary Jo Enyeart   **South Middle School, Downey**

Hot Artichoke Cheese Dip

Serves 6 to 8

1 can (8½ oz.) artichoke hearts, packed in water, drained
1 jar (6 oz.) marinated artichoke hearts, drained
1 can (4 oz.) green chiles, diced
6 tablespoons mayonnaise
1½ to 2 cups cheddar cheese, shredded
tortilla chips

Chop artichokes; mix and distribute evenly over the bottom of a well-greased shallow 7 x 11 inch baking dish. Scatter chiles over artichokes, then carefully spread the mayonnaise over all. Sprinkle cheese over mayonnaise. Cover and heat at 350°F until hot and bubbly, about 15 minutes. Serve with tortilla chips.

Penny Niadna   **Golden West High School, Visalia**

Guacamole Dip
(Avocado sauce with Tomato and Coriander)

Yields about 2 cups

2 large ripe avocados
1 tablespoon onion, finely chopped
1 tablespoon canned serrano chili, rinsed and finely chopped
1 tablespoon fresh coriander (cilantro), finely chopped
1/2 teaspoon salt
1/8 black pepper, freshly ground

Drop tomato into pan of boiling water and remove after 15 seconds. Run tomato under cold water, and with a small, sharp knife, peel. Cut the stem out, then slice the tomato in half crosswise. Squeeze the halves gently to remove the seeds and juices, and chop the tomato fine. Cut the avocados in half. With the tip of a small knife, loosen the seeds and lift them out. Remove any brown tissue-like fibers clinging to the flesh. Strip off the skin with your fingers starting at the narrow or stem end (the dark skinned variey does not peel as easily; use a knife to pull skin away, if necessary). Chop the avocados coarsely; then, in a large mixing bowl, mash with a fork to a smooth puree. Add the chopped onion, chili, tomato, coriander, salt and a few grindings of black pepper, and mix them together gently but thoroughly. Taste for seasoning.

To prevent the guacamole from darkening as it stands, cover it with plastic wrap or aluminum foil and refrigerate until ready to use. Stir before serving and serve either at room temperature or chilled as a dip, or as a salad heaped on chilled lettuce.

Brenda Burke   *Mt. Whitney High, Visalia*

Guacamole La Victoria

Yields 2¼ cups dip

2 avocados, mashed   *1 cup any favorite La Victoria Salsa*
2 tablespoons lemon juice   *2 tablespoons cilantro,*
*   finely chopped*

Sprinkle mashed avocado with lemon juice; mix well. Stir in Salsa and chopped cilantro.

Serve with tortilla chips or vegetable dippers, or use to top broiled steaks or burgers, on sandwiches, or with traditional Mexican dishs.

La Victoria Foods, Inc.   *City of Industry*

Low Cal Mexican Dip

1 can (7 oz.) green chiles, chopped   *3 tablespoons vinegar*
4 green onions, chopped   *2 tablespoons oil*
3 tomatoes, chopped   *salt to taste*
2 cans (4 oz. each) olives, chopped   *¼ teaspoon pepper*

Mix all ingredients together and chill for several hours. Serve as a dip with tortilla chips.

Alcyone Bass   *Hamilton Junior High, Long Beach*

Guacamole Dip

Yields approximately 4 cups

1 package (8 oz.) cream cheese
2 avocados, peeled and mashed
¼ cup onion, finely chopped
1 tablespoon lemon juice
½ teaspoon salt

¼ teaspoon garlic salt
¼ teaspoon tabasco sauce
1 cup chopped tomatoes
corn chips or tortilla chips

Combine softened cream cheese, avocado, onion, lemon juice and seasonings. Mix until well blended. Stir in tomatoes; chill. Serve with chips.

Marie Humphrey   *Grant School, Escondido*

Hot Pepper Nuts

Yields 1 cup

3 tablespoons butter, melted
3 tablespoons soy sauce
½ teaspoon salt
4 to 5 dashes tabasco

dash cayenne pepper
dash cinnamon
3 cups pecan halves

Combine melted butter, soy sauce, tabasco, cayenne pepper and cinnamon. Pour over nuts and spread evenly on baking sheet. Bake 15 minutes at 300°F, stir, spread evenly and continue baking 10 more minutes.

Adjust seasonings to suit your taste. Serve with white wine or pack in jars and give as gifts.

Nancy Hunyadi   *Fullerton High School, Fullerton*

Chili Seasoned Popcorn

Yields 6 to 7 cups

½ cup popping corn
3 tablespoons salad oil
1 teaspoon chili powder

½ teaspoon onion powder
½ teaspoon seasoned salt

Pop popcorn in oil. Mix chili powder, onion powder, and seasoned salt together. Stir and toss into popped corn. Serve and enjoy!

This can be cooled and packed in plastic bags. Perfect "thank you" gifts.

Mary E. Richmond   *San Louis Obispo High School, San Luis Obispo*

Nacho Popcorn

Yields 10 cups

1 teaspoon paprika
½ teapoon each crushed red
  pepper, ground cumin

¼ cup butter, melted
10 cups popped popcorn
⅓ cup parmesan cheese, grated

Stir spices into butter. Toss with popcorn, coating evenly. Sprinkle with cheese.

Ole!

Carl Sheridan   *Dexter Junior High School, Whittier*

Avocado-Shrimp Dip

1/4 teaspoon salt
1/8 teaspoon pepper
1/8 teaspoon garlic powder
1/8 teaspoon dry mustard
2 avocados
¼ cup olive oil or salad oil

2 tablespoons wine vinegar
   (more if you want)
1 tablespoon onion, grated
1 pound small shrimp
paprika
tortilla chips

Mix first 4 ingredients together. Cut avocados in half, scoop out and mash. Keep skins whole. Add all ingredients together, except shrimp. Stir in shrimp. Scoop into empty shells. Garnish with paprika. Serve with tortilla chips.

A real hit at our faculty Christmas party.

Adrienne Steele   *Lee Junior High School, Woodland*

Theresa's Hot Sauce

1 can (28 oz.) whole tomatoes,
   chopped
1 can chiles, diced
1 medium onion, chopped
1 bunch cilantro, chopped
   (key ingredient)

1 teaspoon oregano
2 teaspoons chile peppers, crushed
   (or to taste)
salt
pepper

Mix all ingredients together and chill for several hours.

An original recipe from a former student.

Phyllis Kaylor   *Ray A. Kroc Middle School, San Diego*

Salsa

1 teaspoon canned green chiles, chopped
1 teaspoon canned jalapenos, chopped
   (1½ or 2 teaspoons for very HOT sauce)
⅔ cup tomato sauce
2 teaspoons oil
pinch of garlic powder or garlic salt
pinch of salt
1 tablespoon minced onion, finely chopped

Stir together all ingredients in a small mixing bowl. Cover until used.

The flavor will get better after a few hours.

Kathy Williams   *Jurupa Junior High School, Riverside*

Winter Salsa

1 quart canned tomatoes
1 to 2 dehydrated jalepeno peppers
   or 2 to 3 fresh peppers (this will
   vary with desire for hotness)

4 to 5 cloves minced garlic
½ bunch cilantro
1 onion, minced
1 tablespoon garlic salt

Add all ingredients and blend for 1 to 2 minutes in a blender. Add more peppers or garlic salt to taste.

Dianne Sheats   *Gridley High School, Gridley*

Dorothy's Salsa

Yields about 2 cups

2 cans (4 oz. each) olives, sliced
4 green onions and tops, sliced
1 can (4 oz.) green chiles, diced
3 fresh tomatoes, chopped
1 tablespoon salad oil

3 tablespoons cider vinegar
garlic powder, to taste
1/2 teaspoon oregano, or more
1/4 teaspoon cumin, or more
salt & pepper to taste

Mix everything together and enjoy. Best if made a day or two ahead. Keeps well in the refrigerator — won't last that long!

Absolutely delicious! Goes great on eggs, burritos, whatever!

Nancy Byrum   **Patrick Henry High School, San Diego**

Salsa

Yields approximately 3 cups

3 medium tomatoes
boiling water
1 can (4 oz.) green chiles, diced
2 green onions, finely chopped

1 tablespoon lemon or lime juice
1 garlic clove, minced
1 can (8 oz.) El Pato tomato
   sauce, Mexican hot style

Blanch tomatoes by dipping several seconds in boiling water. Peel tomatoes; then dice. Mix tomatoes with remaining ingredients.

Susan Roa Hope   **Lompoc Valley Middle School, Lompoc**

Salsa

Yields approximately 8 cups

1 can (28 oz.) Ortega green chile
   salsa
1 can (7 oz.) Ortega green chiles,
   diced
1 can El Pato tomato sauce
1 can (8 oz.) tomato sauce
1/2 cup onion, chopped

2 green onions, chopped
1 large fresh tomato, chopped
1 can tomato sauce special
oregano, to taste
garlic, to taste
salt and pepper to taste

Combine all above ingredients. Serve with tortilla chips.

Karen Bennett   **Valencia High School, Placentia**

Salsa Mexicana

Serves 6

1 avocado, diced
1 teaspoon lemon juice
1 small onion, diced
2 medium tomatoes, diced

1 tablespoon fresh cilantro, diced
pinch of salt (to taste)
1 jalapeno pepper, diced

Mix all ingredients together. Chill. Serve as dip for sauce over burritos or taco salad.

Betty Jo Smith   **Tahoe-Truckee High School, Truckee**

Chile Salsa Ⓜ

2 jalapeno chile peppers
2 small yellow chiles
2 long green chiles
1 can (16 oz.) tomatoes, whole
1 onion, cut in quarters

1 clove garlic
1 can (8 oz.) tomato sauce
1 teaspoon vinegar
2 tablespoons fresh cilantro,
   chopped

Place chiles on paper plate with large ones on outside and small ones on the inside. Cover with a paper towel and microwave on HIGH for 6 to 8 minutes, rotating dish at midpoint. Cool and peel. Place all ingredients in food processor or blender and process until it is not quite smooth, but a little chunky. Place in clean jars and refrigerate. Will keep 2 to 3 weeks in the refrigerator.

The vinegar will help preserve the salsa and the cilantro will improve flavor.

Barbara Hansen   **Bishop Amat High, La Puente**

Becky's Salsa

Serves 8

4 large tomatoes, chopped
3 bunches of green onions,
   chopped
1 can (12 oz.) black olives, sliced
1 small can green chiles, diced

1/3 cup parsley or cilantro, minced
1 to 2 teaspoons garlic salt
1/3 cup vinegar
1/2 cup oil
dash of tabasco

Combine first five ingredients in a large bowl. Add garlic salt, vinegar, oil and tabasco. Mix well; taste and adjust seasoning. Refrigerate until served, serve with tortilla chips.

Carolyn Yeutter   **Norco Junior High School, Norco**

Jewell's Salsa Dip

Yields 4 cups

5 medium tomatoes, diced
1 bunch green onions, sliced
1 can (8 oz.) Mexican-style hot
   tomato sauce
1 can (8 oz.) green chile salsa

1 can (4 oz.) black olives, diced
dash tabasco sauce
salt & pepper to taste
garlic powder to taste
tortilla chips

Combine tomatoes, green onions, hot tomato sauce, green chile salsa, olives and tabasco sauce. Add salt, pepper and garlic powder to taste. Refrigerate at least 3 hours. Drain, if desired. Serve with chips.

Jewell Lasseter has satisfied many hungry snackers over the years with this zesty dip.

Clyle Alt   **Bell Gardens High School, Bell Gardens**

Mexi-Dip

Serves 6

1 can (16 oz.) refried beans or
  2 cans (9 oz. each) bean dip
1 cup green onions, chopped
¾ cup salsa
2 large avocados, mashed
1 cup sour cream

1 cup monterey jack cheese,
  shredded
1 cup cheddar cheese, shredded
4 oz. black olives, chopped,
  optional
tortilla chips or raw vegetables

Spread the refried beans or bean dip on the bottom of a 9 x 13 inch pan. Sprinkle the green onions over the beans. Spread the salsa evenly over the green onions. Combine the mashed avocado and sour cream. Spread the mixture on top of the salsa. Sprinkle the cheese on the top. If you want, garnish with black olives. Chill and serve with chips or raw vegetables.

Sally Spieker   *Tehachapi High School, Tehachapi*

Carne Asada Marinade

Serves 6 to 8

2 tablespoons olive oil
¼ cup orange juice
¼ cup tomato juice
2 teaspoons lime juice
1 teaspoon paprika

1 teaspoon cumin seed
1 teaspoon oregano
½ teaspoon red chile pepper
2 teaspoons garlic salt

Mix all the above ingredients. Pour over London broil steak and refrigerate at least six hours.

Lou Ann Walling   *Meadowbrook Middle School, Poway*

Wilda's Jalapeno Pepper Jelly

¾ cup green bell peppers,
  finely chopped
½ cup whole green jalapeno chile
  peppers, seeded and chopped
1½ cups cider vinegar

6 cups sugar
6 oz. Certo
green food coloring
½ can (canned) hot pepper,
  fresh burned
paraffin

Place green peppers and jalapenos in an electric blender with ½ cup vinegar. Blend until smooth. Pour mixture into a 4 quart kettle. Rinse blender with remaining vinegar and add it to pan. Stir in sugar. Bring mixture to a hard rolling boil that you can't stir down. Boil one minute. Remove from heat and cool to lukewarm. Skim off any foam and strain, if necessary. Stir in pectin, food coloring and hot pepper. Pour into 6 pint jars. Top with paraffin. Keeps indefinitely in the refrigerator.

Elaine Golden   *Rancho-Starbuck Junior High School, Whittier*

Mexican Chocolate

Serves 20 to 25

5 quarts milk
25 ounces semisweet chocolate squares
15 cinnamon sticks
1 tablespoon plus 1 teaspoon vanilla

Combine milk, semisweet chocolate and cinnamon sticks in saucepan. Cook and stir just until chocolate melts. Remove from heat. Remove cinnamon and stir in vanilla. Beat with electric beater until frothy. Serve immediately. Place cinnamon sticks into mugs and pour drink in.

Great idea for whenever a group gathers.

Vicki Warner-Huggins   **Placer High School, Auburn**

Sober Sangria

Yields 8 servings

1 pint cranberry juice
1 can (6 oz.) frozen orange juice
2 tablespoons lemon juice
1 quart raspberry or strawberry soda, chilled

Combine cranberry juice, orange juice reconstituted according to package directions and lemon juice. Chill. Just before serving add soda.

This can be dressed up with a few fresh orange slices and lemon slices.

Madelyn V. Fielding   **Jordan High School, Long Beach**

Margaritas

1 shot Triple Sec
2 shots tequila
1 can (6 oz.) frozen lemonade
1 can (6 oz.) water

Pour into blender, then fill blender with crushed ice and blend until smooth.

Sheryl Malone   **Poway High School, Poway**

Kahlua

6 cups water
½ cup instant coffee
6 cups sugar
1.75 liter vodka or brandy
½ cup vanilla

Bring water, coffee and sugar to a boil. Simmer for 2 hours. When cool, add vodka and vanilla.

Enjoy!

Carl Sheridan   **Dexter Junior High School, Whittier**

Salads

Chicken Taco Salad

Serves 5

Salad Ingredients:

1 head lettuce
2 green onions, chopped
1 cup canned kidney beans,
   drained
2 tomatoes, sliced
1 bag tortilla chips
2 cups cheese, grated

Meat Dressing:

3 cups cooked chicken, diced
1 cup tomato sauce
1 cup chicken broth
¼ cup water
1 tablespoon instant minced onion
⅛ teaspoon garlic powder
⅛ teaspoon ground cumin
⅛ teaspoon black pepper
1 teaspoon chili powder
1 teaspoon salt

In a frying pan, simmer all meat dressing ingredients for 20 minutes. Let cool 10 minutes.

On individual plates, mound tortilla chips. Layer with lettuce, onions, kidney beans, tomatoes, on top of chips. Spoon hot meat sauce on top of salad. Grate cheese on top. Serve.

Variations: Substitute 1 lb. ground beef in place of chicken. Substitute beef broth for chicken broth for beef taco salad. Try a variety of salad greens, olives, etc. Add variety and eye appeal.

April Herman   *Townsend Junior High School, Chino*

Tortilla Chip Salad

Serves 8

½ head iceburg lettuce
½ lb. ground beef
dash of garlic powder, chili powder,
   cayenne red pepper, seasoned salt
2 drops red pepper hot sauce
1 can kidney beans, save ¼ cup liquid
2 tomatoes, cut in chunks
1 medium orange, sliced and
   segmented

½ to 1 cup chopped: cucumber,
   green pepper,
   raw and peeled jicama
1 cup chile salsa
2 teaspoons pickle relish
½ bag tortilla chips
2 to 4 oz. cheddar cheese, shredded
½ cup onion, chopped

Wash lettuce, tear into bite-size pieces; chill. Cook and stir ground beef in a large skillet until brown; drain. Stir in seasonings, kidney beans and liquid heat to boiling. Reduce heat, simmer uncovered for 15 minutes, stirring occasionally. Cool 10 minutes. Prepare fresh produce, combine with greens in a large bowl. Mix chile salsa and pickle relish together.

*Note: All of the above may be done ahead of time to help with our busy schedules.

When ready, toss greens, produce, salsa, chips, cheese and onion together. Pour ground beef mixture over salad, toss gently. Serve immediately.

While I taught a Foods class to a group of ESL students, mostly Vietnamese and Cambodian who were very new to our county, I had them prepare this dish to expose them to our native foods, and I found they loved it! I've never had a dissatisifed student yet!

D. Yamamoto/Deanna Taylor   Mesa Verde High School, Citrus Heights

Ensalada De Napoles
(Cactus Salad)

Serves 4

1 can cactus (nopalitos)
3 tablespoons vinegar
2 tablespoons salad oil
salt
fresh ground pepper

2 tomatoes, sliced
1 large white onion, sliced
6 tablespoons Mexican cheese,
    grated (can use Monterey jack)

Rinse the cactus pieces **very well** and place them in a salad bowl. Add the vinegar and oil. Sprinkle with salt and pepper. Mix thoroughly. Garnish the bowl with slices of tomato and onin. Sprinkle with more salt and pepper. Garnish with grated cheese. Serve cold.

This is a different type salad to serve with Mexican meals. Recipe from Juan J. Denis, an instructor at California State University, Sacramento.

Gloria Walker   Casa Roble Fundamental High School, Orangevale

Tam's Taco Salad

Serves 4 to 6

¾ lb. lean ground beef
1 jar medium hot salsa
1 head iceberg lettuce, shredded
1 bag Fritos corn chips, crunched

½ lb. cheddar cheese, shredded
2 tomatoes, chopped
sour cream
sliced olives

Brown ground beef, drain off fat. Add salsa and heat through. Shred lettuce, put on plates and layer beef mixture, crunched Fritos, shredded cheese and chopped tomatoes. Top with sour cream and sliced olives. Great tasting — quick and easy!

Marilyn Tam   Orange Glen High School, Escondido

La Victoria's Taco Salad

Serves 6

1 lb. ground beef
1 teaspoon salt
½ teaspoon pepper
1 small head iceberg lettuce,
    torn in pieces
1 cup grated cheddar cheese
1 can (15 oz.) kidney beans,
    drained and lightly rinsed

½ cup green onion, chopped
1 tomato, cut in wedges
1 small avocado, sliced
½ to ¾ cup oil and vinegar or
    Italian salad dressing
¾ cup La Victoria Green Taco
    Sauce, or desired Salsa

Brown ground beef; drain off fat. Season with salt and pepper.

To assemble salads, layer lettuce, cheese, meat, beans, olives, green onion, tomato wedges, and avocado onto each plate.

Serve salads with dressing and Taco Sauce or Salsa.

La Victoria Foods, Inc.   City of Industry

Prawns with Salsa, page 96

Super Nachos, page 8

Hearty Black Bean Soup, page 35

Guacamole La Victoria, page 17

Ensalada De Calabacita (Zucchini Salad)

Serves 8

4 cups zucchini, sliced
1 cup white wine vinegar
¾ cup olive oil
2 tablespoons sugar
1 clove garlic, minced
1 teaspoon dried basil, crushed

1 teaspoon salt
few dashes pepper
lettuce
¼ cup green onion, sliced
2 medium tomatoes,
    cut in this wedges

Cook zucchini in small amount of boiling salted water for about 3 minutes or until crisp tender; drain. Arrange half the zucchini in a single layer in a 10 x 6 x 2 inch dish.

In a screw top jar, combine vinegar, oil, sugar, garlic, basil, salt, and pepper. Cover and shake well. Pour **half** the dressing over zucchini in dish. Top with the remaining zucchini and dressing. **Cover and chill overnight.**

To serve, drain zucchini, reserve ¼ cup dressing. Arrange zucchini on lettuce lined plate; top with sliced green onion. Arrange tomato wedges around zucchini. Drizzle with reserved dressing.

Linda Robinson   *Sinaloa Junior High School, Simi Valley*

Orange Bright Salad

Serves 4

1 head romaine lettuce
6 medium to large mushrooms
1 teaspoon fine herbs
3 medium oranges

1 small spanish onion
⅓ cup sliced almonds
1 tablespoon granulated sugar

Wash, dry and tear romaine into bite-sized pieces. Wash, dry and slice mushrooms and toss with lettuce. Add fine herbs and toss again. Place in the refrigerator to chill while preparing the rest of the ingredients and the salad dressing. Peel oranges, removing entire skin and white membrane. Slice into ¼ inch slices. Peel and slice as thin as possible the spanish onion. Place almonds and sugar in a heavy skillet. Toss and heat slowly, stirring constantly. Sugar should be melted, forming a glaze over the almonds. Cool.

Dressing:

2 tablespoons vinegar
4 tablespoons salad oil
1 tablespoon granulated sugar

1 tablespoons fresh parsley, chopped
dash seasoned pepper
dash tabasco sauce

Prepare dressing by mixing all the ingredients in a glass bottle. Shake before using. Prepare salad for serving by placing orange slices around the outside edge of a salad bowl, alternating with spanish onion rings. Crumble almonds and sprinkle over top. Drizzle dressing over salad and serve immediately.

Mary E. Richmond   *San Luis Obispo High School, San Luis Obispo*

Ensalada de Naranjas *(nah-rahn-has)*
(Orange Salad)

Serves 8

5 large oranges
1 white onion, thinly sliced
⅓ cup salad oil
¼ cup wine vinegar

1 teaspoon sugar
¼ teaspoon salt
½ teaspoon chili powder
paprika
crisp lettuce, optional

Peel oranges, cutting away white membrane, and slice. Arrange orange and onion slices alternately in a bowl. Mix the oil, vinegar, sugar, salt, chili powder; pour over the salad. Sprinkle with paprika. If you wish, serve on crisp lettuce.

This version of orange and onion salad has chili powder seasonings.

Ramona Anderson   *Mira Mesa High School, San Diego*

Mexican Crab Salad

Serves 6

1 lb. imitation crab
1 pint fresh salsa
2 avocados

1 large tomato
lettuce leaves
tortilla chips

Dice in bite size pieces crab, avocado and tomato. Four to eight hours before serving, mix all ingredients except lettuce. Arrange on lettuce leaves and garnish with chips.

Fast but elegant.

Lynda Ruth   *La Mirada High School, La Mirada*

Marinated Tomato Salad
with Salad Dressing Verde

Serves 6

1 zucchini or cucumber,
   thinly sliced
1 green bell pepper, slivered
1 small onion, thinly sliced
2 medium tomatoes,
   cut into thin wedges

½ cup ripe olives
½ cup salad oil
¼ cup La Victoria Green Taco
   Sauce
¼ cup fresh lemon juice or vinegar
½ teaspoon salt
½ teaspoon garlic powder

Combine vegetables together in a large salad bowl.

Prepare dressing by combining oil, Green Taco Sauce, lemon juice or vinegar, salt, and garlic powder in a large shaker jar. Cover and shake well to blend.

Drizzle dressing over salad; toss gently to coat with dressing. Cover and chill 1 hour before serving to blend flavors. Makes 1 cup dressing.

La Victoria Foods, Inc.   *City of Industry*

Shrimp Salad

Serves 6

2 pounds shrimp, peeled
¾ cup mayonnaise
1 small can green chiles, chopped
1 small clove garlic, minced

lettuce or romaine leaves
1 canned jalapeno chiles,
  seeded and chopped
  (optional for hotter taste)

Cook shrimp in boiling salted water until they turn pink. Drain. Rinse with cold water to cool. De-vein. Cut into bite-size pieces unless shrimp are very small. Combine with other ingredients and serve on lettuce leaves.

Joyce Grohman   *Bellflower High School, Bellflower*

Salad Burrito

Serves 6 to 8

6 limes
1 teaspoon garlic, crushed
½ yellow onion
½ teaspoon fine herbs
½ teaspoon cumin
2 to 3 lbs. sirloin tip

1 avocado
3 tomatoes
5 cucumbers
2 green onions
½ green pepper
¼ cup cilantro
1 package flour tortillas

24 hours before serving: Prepare a marinade of limes, garlic, onion, herbs and cumin. Cut meat into ½ to ¾ inch strips and marinate, turning occasionally.

3 to 4½ hours before serving: Prepare salad: Dice up avocado, tomatoes, cucumbers, onion and pepper and minced cilantro. Mix together; cover and refrigerate. Add additional seasonings for personal taste.

Prepare BBQ: Warm tortillas in the oven at 250°F. Cook meat. Set out salad, tortillas, meat. Either fill ahead or have each person fill their own. May serve along with your favorite salsa, cheese or sour cream. Be creative! Good for parties or large crowds.

Alternative: Instead of BBQ, bake in the oven at 325°F for 45 minutes to 1 hour, turn in the juices.

Dixie Neal   *Granite Hills High School, El Cajon*

Spanish Gazpacho Salad Mold

Serves 6 to 8

1 envelopes plain gelatin
1½ cups tomato juice
2 tablespoons wine vinegar
1 large tomato, seeded & chopped
1 cucumber, peeled & chopped

2 tablespoons green chiles, chopped
¼ cup green onions, sliced
1 clove garlic, pressed
¼ teaspoon salt
⅛ teaspoon pepper
greens

Soften gelatin in ¼ cup juice. Heat remaining juice. Add softened gelatin and stir until thoroughly dissolved. Add vinegar, vegetables, and seasoning. Pour into 1 quart mold. Chill overnight. Unmold on a platter lined with greens.

Ramona Anderson   *Mira Mesa High School, San Diego*

Soups

Gazpacho (Soup)

1 cup hothouse cucumber, sliced
4 tomatoes, peeled and seeded
1 teaspoon salt
1 teaspoon red wine vinegar
4 tablespoons fresh lime juice
2 cloves garlic, chopped

1 teaspoon worcestershire sauce
1/2 teaspoon tabasco
1/3 cup each for garnish:
  green bell pepper, minced
  celery and cucumber, diced
1 tablespoon cilantro, chopped

Combine all the soup ingredients in a blender or food processor, fitted with the steel blade, and process to a smooth consistency. Chill the soup until it is ice cold. After it is chilled, taste the soup for seasoning and adjust with more lime juice, worcestershire sauce and tabasco as needed. Garnish each serving.

Kathy Stanger   *El Dorado High School, Placentia*

Sopa de Melon Escribe (Cantaloupe Soup)

Serves 6

1/2 cup half and half
1 cup potato, cooked,
  peeled and diced
3 cups cantaloupe,
  peeled and diced

1/4 cup dry sherry
pinch of salt
optional:
  nutmeg
  lime, sliced

Place the half and half, potato, and cantaloupe in the blender. Blend to a smooth puree. Stir in sherry. Season to taste.

Serve chilled. If desired, garnish with a sprinkle of nutmeg or lime slice.

Joyce Grohmann   *Bellflower High School, Bellflower*

Taco Beef Soup

Serves 6 to 8

1/3 lb. ground beef
1/4 cup onions, chopped
1 cup water
1 can (12 oz.) stewed tomatoes
1 can (12 oz.) kidney beans
1 can (6 oz.) tomato sauce
Taco Seasoning Mix:

taco seasoning mix
  (ingredients listed below)
1/3 small avocado
2 oz. cheddar cheese, shredded
1/4 cup dairy sour cream

1 1/2 teaspoons instant minced onion
1/2 teaspoon chili powder
1 1/2 teaspoon ground cumin
1 1/2 teaspoon salt

1/2 teaspoon crushed hot red
  pepper flakes
1/4 teaspoon instant minced garlic
1/4 teaspoon cornstarch
3/4 teaspoon oregano, crushed well

Brown beef and onion in skillet. Drain off excess fat. Put in saucepan with water. Add stewed tomatoes, kidney beans, tomato sauce and taco seasoning mix. Simmer, covered for 15 minutes. Add avocado. Top with sour cream.

Courtesy of Netta Roberts, formerly in our Home Ec Dept.

Marcia Nye   *Woodrow Wilson High School, Long Beach*

Sopa de Aguacate *(Avocado Cream Soup)*

Serves 8

3 large ripe avocados
1½ cups cream
6 cups chicken stock
¼ cup cooking sherry (optional)

1 teaspoon salt
½ teaspoon white pepper
3 tortillas, quartered and
   fried until crisp

Puree avocados with cream, using a food processor or a blender. Meanwhile bring the chicken stock to a boil. Reduce heat to low and stir in the avocado-cream puree. Add the sherry, if desired, and the salt and pepper and heat to simmer. Adjust seasoning and serve with the tortilla quarters. Or as a variation, this may be served cold.

Gwenn Jensen   *Mira Mesa High School, San Diego*

Albondigas Soup

Serves 10

Broth:

5 cans (10½ oz. each) beef bouillon
1 quart water
1 to 2 cans (7 oz. each) green
   chile salsa
1 onion, chopped
1 can (28 oz.) tomatoes
½ teaspoon basil
½ teaspoon oregano
1 teaspoon salt
¼ teaspooon pepper
½ cup rice

Meatballs:

1 lb. ground chuck
¼ lb. pork sausage
1 onion, chopped
1 egg, beaten
½ teaspoon salt
¼ teaspoon pepper
¼ teaspoon garlic powder
¼ cup milk
¼ cup basil
½ cup cornmeal

Mix first 9 ingredients to make broth. Bring to a boil and simmer 20 minutes. Combine ingredients for meatballs. Mix well and form into tiny bite size meatballs. Add meatballs and rice to broth. Simmer very slowly covered for 1 to 1½ hours.

Best I've ever tasted!

Charla Rayl   *El Toro High School, El Toro*

Taco Soup

Serves 4 to 6

1 lb. ground beef
1 onion, chopped
1½ cups water
1 can (16 oz.) stewed tomatoes
1 can (16 ox.) chili beans
1 can (8 oz.) tomato sauce

2 tablespoons taco seasoning mix
sour cream
corn chips
avocado chunks
shredded cheese

Brown ground beef and onions. Drain off all fat. Combine water, stewed tomatoes, chili beans, tomato sauce, taco seasoning mix. Add to meat mixture. Simmer in a large kettle for ½ hour. Pour into bowls and garnish with the toppings.

Barbara Ford   *Cope Junior High School, Redlands*

Meatball Soup

Serves 4

3 onions
3 tablespoons bacon grease
1 can (16 oz.) tomatoes
1 can (4 oz.) green chiles, chopped
1 quart water
1 can beef bouillon

salt and pepper to taste
1/4 teaspoon cumin powder
fresh cilantro leaves, cut up
3 raw tortillas
1 lb. extra lean ground beef
1 egg
1 clove garlic, crushed

Dice onions and saute in bacon grease. Add tomatoes, chiles, water, bouillon, salt and pepper to taste, cumin and cilantro leaves. Cook at least 30 minutes after mixture is simmering (more water may be added if soup become to thick).

Cut tortillas into tiny slivers. Work into ground meat with egg and garlic. Shape into tiny balls about the size of a marble. Drop meatballs into simmering soup. When meatballs float, the soup is ready to serve.

Leota Hill   Saddleback High School, Santa Ana

Easy Taco Soup

Serves 8 to 10

1 onion, finely chopped
1 lb. lean ground beef
1 large can of each: tomatoes
    tomato sauce, and refried beans

1 package taco seasoning
1 lb. jack cheese
1 large package corn chips
1 carton (8 oz.) sour cream

In a large pot or skillet saute onion and beef until meat is well browned. Add tomatoes, tomato sauce, beans and seasonings. Add some water, to make desired thickness. Cook 20 minutes, low. Serving: Mugs or bowls; place chips in bowl; add soup; top with sour cream and sprinkle with cheese. YUM!

I use this soup for large groups. It's easy, tastes great, and people come back for more. I used to make as a taco dip and needed a soup for a church activity; hence, add some water and voila "taco soup."

Beret R. Mason   Ganesha High School, Pomona

Mexican Bean Soup

Serves 4

4 slices bacon, diced
3/4 cup onion, chopped
3/4 cup celery, chopped
1 clove garlic, minced
1 can (4 oz.) green chiles, chopped
1 can (16 oz.) refried beans

1/4 teaspoon black pepper
1/4 teaspoon chili powder
few drops hot pepper sauce
1 can (13 oz.) chicken broth
cheddar cheese, shredded
tortilla chips

In a 2 quart saucepan, cook bacon until crisp. Add onion, celery and garlic. Cover and cook over low heat, stirring occasionally, 10 minutes, or until vegetables are tender but not brown. Add green chiles, beans, pepper, chili powder, hot pepper sauce and chicken broth and stir. Bring to a boil. Ladle into individual bowls. Pass cheese and tortilla chips to add as desired.

Eleanor Magorien   El Toro High School, El Toro

Chile/Cheese/Tortilla Soup

Serves 6

1 small onion, chopped
2 tablespoons oil
2½ cups canned tomatoes,
  chopped
3 cups chicken broth
1 can (4 oz.) Ortega chiles,
  chopped

½ teaspoon cumin
1 teaspoon salt
⅛ teaspoon pepper
3 potatoes, peeled and chopped
2 cups cheddar cheese, grated
3 cups tortilla strips (corn)

Saute onion in oil until soft. Add tomatoes, chicken broth, Ortega chiles, cumin, salt, pepper and potatoes. Cook covered over medium heat until potatoes are tender. Add cheese and corn tortilla strips to soup just before serving. Cook for 40 minutes over medium heat.

A favorite soup from my Foods classes.

Nancy Hunyadi   *Fullerton High School, Fullerton*

Mexicali Vegetable Soup

Serves 12

2 tablespoon cooking oil
2 garlic cloves, minced
1 cup cooked diced ham
1 cup chopped onion
1 cup sliced celery
1 lb. green beans, bias-sliced
  1 inch thick
2 carrots, peeled and bias-sliced

4 cups chicken broth
2 cans (28 oz. each) enchilada sauce
2 zucchini, sliced
2 yellow summer squash, sliced
½ cup parsley, minced
Garnishes: La Victoria Salsa,
  fresh cilantro, zucchini sticks,
  sour cream, sliced avocado

In a large stock pot or Dutch oven heat oil. Saute garlic, ham, onion, and celery till tender. Add beans, carrots, chicken broth, and enchilada sauce. Bring mixture to boiling; reduce heat. Cover and simmer 20 minutes. Stir in zucchini and yellow squash; simmer 10 minutes more. Stir in parsley; serve with desired garnishes.

La Victoria Foods, Inc.   *City of Industry*

Gazpacho

Serves 5 to 6

1 clove garlic, halved
1 package Lawry's Mexican Rice
  Seasoning Mix
1½ cups tomato juice
1½ lbs. fresh tomatoes
¼ cup green pepper, minced

1 medium cucumber, peeled and
  chopped
¼ cup onion, minced
2 tablespoons olive oil
1 tablespoon vinegar
Lawry's Seasoned Pepper

Rub large bowl with garlic. Empty Mexican rice seasoning into bowl. Add tomato juice and stir thoroughly. Peel tomatoes, remove cores and chop into small pieces. Add tomatoes, green pepper, cucumbers and onion to seasoned tomato juice. Add olive oil and vinegar; mix thoroughly. Chill well before serving. Add a sprinkle of seasoned pepper.

Dorothy Wilson   *Dale Junior High School, Anaheim*

Sopa De Papas Con Chile with Verde y Questo

(Potato Soup with Green Chile and Cheese)

Serves 4 to 6

*2 green onions or 1/2 small onion,
    chopped
1 clove garlic, minced
1 small can green chiles, chopped
1 tablespoon oil
1 medium tomato, chopped*

*1 quart beef or chicken stock
3 medium potatoes, cubed
pinch of dry oregano
3 or 4 oz. jack cheese, grated
salt and pepper to taste*

Saute the onion, garlic, and chiles in the oil until the onion is soft. Add the tomato and simmer several minutes. Add the hot stock and the potatoes and cook. Add the oregano, salt, pepper and the grated cheese. Heat gently and serve hot.

Joyce Grohmann   *Bellflower High School, Bellflower*

Hearty Black Bean and Rice Condiment Soup

Serves 12

*8 oz. dried black beans
1 tablespoon cooking oil
1 small onion, chopped
1 carrot, diced
1 stalk celery, sliced
2 to 3 cloves garlic, minced
3 cups chicken or beef broth
3 cups bean broth,
    or chicken or beef broth
2 can (28 oz.) La Victoria
    Enchilada Sauce
1 lb. ham hocks, cracked
    (optional)*

*1 cup uncooked brown rice
2 tablespoons vinegar
    or lemon juice
1 bay leaf
1 teaspoon ground cumin
    (optional)
1/2 teaspoon dried oregano,
    crushed (optional)
Garnishes: La Victoria Nacho
    Sliced Jalapenos, sliced radishes,
    cilantro or parsley sprigs,
    sour cream or yogurt, or corn
    tortillas, warmed and rolled*

Rinse and sort beans; place beans and water to cover in a 5 quart Dutch oven. Soak overnight. Cover and bring to boiling; reduce heat. Simmer 30 minutes or till most of the water is absorbed.

Meanwhile, heat oil in a 4 quart saucepan over medium heat. Add onion, carrots, celery and garlic; saute till onion is tender. Add remaining ingredients except beans and garnishes; simmer 20 to 30 minutes more.

Process 2 cups of the beans and 1/2 cup of the soup in blender or food processor till smooth; add to soup along with remaining beans. Heat through. Serve soup with garnishes.

La Victoria Foods, Inc.   *City of Industry*

Sopa Pollo Mexicana (Mexican Chicken Soup)

Serves 10

1 4½ to 5 lb. stewing chicken, cut up
6 cups water
3 to 4 onion slices
3 stalks celery, cut up
1 teaspoon salt
⅛ teaspoon pepper
1 can (16 oz.) tomatoes, cut up

3 medium carrots, thinly sliced (1½ cups)
1 medium onion, chopped (½ cup)
4 teaspoons instant chicken bouillan granules
1 small zucchini, thinly sliced
1 cup frozen peas
1 small avocado, seeded, peeled and sliced

In large kettle combine chicken, water, onion slices, celery, salt and pepper. Simmer, covered, for 2 hours or until chicken is tender. Remove chicken from broth, discarding vegetables, and return broth to kettle. Add undrained tomatoes, sliced carrots, chopped onion and bouillon granules; simmer, covered, for 30 minutes or until the carrots are tender. Meanwhile when chicken is cool enough to handle, remove skin and bones from chicken; discard skin and bones. Cube chicken, add to broth along with zucchini and peas. Cover and simmer 10 to 15 minutes longer or until vegetables are tender. Just before serving, garnish with avocado slices.

Lorraine S. Pepper   *Oceanside High School, Oceanside*

Breads & Things

Mexican Corn Bread

Serves 8

1 cup cornmeal
½ teaspoon salt
½ teaspoon soda
1 cup milk
1 small can cream-style corn

½ pound cheese, grated
2 eggs
1 medium onion, chopped
1 or more jalapeno peppers,
    chopped
¼ to ½ cup bacon drippings

Mix cornmeal, salt and soda. Add milk, corn, grated cheese and eggs. Stir well. Add onions, peppers and bacon drippings. Pour into a greased pan and bake for 1 hour at 350°F.

Dorothy Wilson   *Dale Junior High School, Anaheim*

Ripe Olive Bread

Yields 1 loaf

3 eggs, beaten
2 tablespoons sugar
1 teaspoon salt
3 tablespoons olive oil

3 cups pitted ripe olives, chopped
    (2 6 oz. cans)
3 cups sifted flour
1 tablespoon baking powder
¾ cup milk

Beat eggs with sugar, salt and oil. Stir in olives. Sift flour with baking powder and add alternately with milk to other ingredients. Stir gently until just blended. Pour mixture into a well greased loaf pan (9 x 5 x 3 inches). **Let stand 30 minues.** Bake in pre-heated oven for 1 to 1½ hours until bread tests done. **Do not serve warm.** Bread improves upon standing.

This may not be strictly Mexican, but it goes well with Mexican dishes, especially seafood.

Linda Robinson   *Sinaloa Junior High, Simi Valley*

Navajo Frybread

Serves 12

1 tablespoon shortening
3¾ cups all purpose flour
1 cup cornmeal
1 tablespoon baking powder
1 teaspoon salt
1 cup milk
1 cup water

oil for frying
2 cans (15 oz.) chili beans, heated
1½ cups iceberg lettuce, shredded
1 cup tomatoes, finely chopped
1 cup cheddar cheese, shredded

Cut shortening into combined dry ingredients until mixture resembles coarse crumbs. Stir in milk and water. Knead dough on lightly floured surface about 5 times. Roll out dough on lightly floured surface into 1/8 inch thickness. Cut into 5 inch squares. Fry in 1 inch of hot oil (375°F) until golden brown on each side, turning once. Drain on absorbent paper. Spoon hot chili over each frybread. Top with lettuce, tomato and cheese.

Edith Novascone   *Burroughs High School, Ridgecrest*

Sweet Buns (Pan Dulce)

Yields 1½ dozen

1 package yeast,
  dry or compressed
¾ cup warm water
3½ cups all purpose flour
¾ cup sugar

½ teaspoon salt
3 tablespoons butter or margarine,
  melted
2 eggs slightly beaten
cinnamon flavored topping

Dissolve the yeast in the ¾ cup water. Sift flour, measure sift again with the sugar and salt into a bowl. Add the yeast mixture, butter, and eggs; beat until smooth. Place dough in a greased bowl, cover and let rise in a warm place until doubled in bulk, about 1½ hours. Stir down, turn out onto a lightly floured board and knead until smooth and elastic. Pinch off pieces of dough and shape into smooth rounded balls about 1¼ inches in diameter.

Place balls of dough on a greased baking sheet, about 2 inches apart. With palm of your hand, press each ball down, flattening it slightly. Gently spread about 1 tablespoon topping on each bun, let buns rise until doubled in bulk, about 30 minutes. Bake in a 400°F oven for 10 minutes or until lightly browned. Serve warm.

Cinnamon Flavored Topping:

1 cup sugar
1 cup sifted flour
½ cup butter or margarine, melted

1 egg, slightly beaten
1 teaspoon cinnamon
dash of salt

Blend all ingredients together in order listed.

To freeze these buns, cool thoroughly, then wrap tightly. To reheat, place buns on baking sheet in a 400°F oven for 3 to 5 minutes.

Eudora Mitchell   **Norwalk High School, Norwalk**

Fiesta Rolls

Yields 12

12 small french rolls
1½ cups (about 6 oz.) sharp
  cheddar cheese, shredded
1 can (4½ ounces) ripe olives,
  chopped
½ cup green peppers,
  finely chopped

2 green onions, finely sliced
2 hard cooked eggs, chopped
1 can (8 oz.) tomato sauce
½ cup butter or margarine, melted
2 tablespoons white wine vinegar
½ teaspoon Dijon mustard
½ teaspoon salt

Using a grapefruit knife or other small sharp knife, cut a 1 inch cone shaped plug from one end of each roll; set plug aside and scoop out most of the inside of the roll (save crumbs for other uses). Combine cheese, drained olives, green peppers, onions, eggs, tomato sauce, butter, vinegar, mustard and salt. Stuff mixture into scooped out rolls; replace plug and tightly wrap each roll in foil.

Bake wrapped rolls in a 350°F oven for 50 minutes.

Sydney Fox   **Orange Glen High School, Escondido**

Sopaipillas (deep fried bread)

Serves 6 to 8

3 cups flour, sifted
1 teaspoon salt
1 tablespoon baking powder
¼ cup shortening

1 egg
water (enough to hold mixture
 together)
1 quart oil

Sift to mix flour, salt and baking powder. Cut in shortening. Add egg and water. Mix well (dough must be moist and pliable, not dry). Roll out on floured board 1/8 inch thick. Cut into small squares or triangles. Deep fry in hot fat.

This recipe was given to me by the head cook at "Bobby's Restaurant" in Santa Rosa, New Mexico, while on vacation 15 years ago.

Angie Garrett   *Tenaya Middle School, Fresno*

Corn Tortillas

Yields 12 tortillas

1⅔ cups masa harina *
⅓ cup sifted all purpose flour
¾ cup teaspoon salt

In a large bowl, combine masa, flour and salt. Add 1 cup water, stirring until mixture is completely moistened. Use more water if necessary. Form into a large ball.

On lightly floured surface, knead or work dough until it is no longer sticky — about 5 minutes. Divide into 12 equal balls and let dough rest 20 minutes at room temperature. On floured surface, roll out each ball into a 6 inch circle. With a paring knife and using a 6 inch saucer as a guide, trim evenly.

On a heated, ungreased griddle or large skillet, cook the tortillas for 1 minute, then turn and cook 1 minute on the other side. Allow to cool, then keep covered with a damp towel.

*This corn flour is available in specialty food stores or is available nationally from Quaker Oats.

Sydney Fox   *Orange Glen High School, Escondido*

Flour Tortillas

Yields approximately 30

6 cups flour
2 tablespoons baking powder
1 tablespoon salt

1 cup lard or shortening
2 to 2¼ cups hot water

Combine the flour, baking powder, and salt in a large bowl. Cut in the shortening. Add hot water. You may add more water if the dough is too dry. Knead for 3 minutes. Let dough set for at least 20 minutes.

Form into small balls. Roll each into a circle. Heat griddle or frying pan to medium high temperature. Place tortilla on hot griddle. Cook just until bubbles appear all over surface. Turn and cook other side until lightly brown. Transfer cooked tortillas to cloth-lined basket and cover to keep warm.

Betty Wells   *Oroville High School, Oroville*

White Flour Tortillas

Yields 2 to 3 dozen

4 cups flour
2 teaspoons salt
2 teaspoons powdered milk,
  optional

2 teaspoons baking powder
6 tablespoons shortening
1½ cups lukewarm water

Mix dry ingredients. Add shortening and mix thoroughly. Add water and mix well.

Shape dough into egg size balls, and place on floured board. Cover with waxed paper and let stand for 20 minutes. Dust board with flour and roll out dough, round and paper thin.

Place on hot grill. Cook 1 to 1½ minutes on each side.

Cool, place in a plastic bag and refrigerate.

Sally Spieker   *Tehachapi High School, Tehachapi*

Vegetables & Fixin's

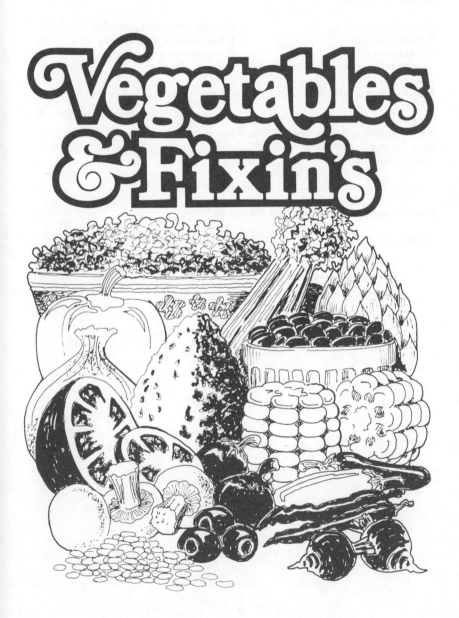

Seasoned Refried Beans

Yields about 4 cups

2 cans (17 oz.) refried beans
1/4 teaspoons Lawry's Garlic Powder with Parsley
1 tablespoon Lawry's Minced Onion with Green Onion Flakes
2 1/2 cups cheddar cheese, grated

Combine all ingredients in a 2 1/2 quart casserole dish. Cover and bake in a 350°F oven for 25 minutes or until beans are hot and cheese is thoroughly melted.

Dorothy Wilson   **Dale Junior High School, Anaheim**

Colache (Mexican Succotash)

Serves 6

1 pound zucchini	1 small onion
4 ears fresh corn (1 can	1/4 cup butter
(niblets may be substituted)	salt and pepper to taste
1 pound tomatoes	1 cup jack cheese, grated

Cut zucchini in small pieces. Cut kernels from corn cobs. Peel and cube tomatoes. Cook onion in butter until lightly colored. Add vegetables, salt and pepper. Cover and simmer about 15 minutes or until vegetables are tender. Shake pan occasionally to prevent scorching.

Transfer to heated serving dish. Top with jack cheese. Heat of vegetables will melt cheese. Serve at once.

Squash haters will like this if the vegetables are not overdone. Cheese amount may be increased. Garlic may be added with onion for a change of pace. My family prefers omitting the tomato (which is traditional) and increasing the amount of corn.

Betsy Cosart   **Monache High School, Porterville**

Company Carrots

Serves 8

2 bunches carrots, about 1 1/2 lbs.	salt to taste
1/2 cup cooking liquid from carrots	1/4 cup fine cracker crumbs
1/2 cup mayonnaise	2 tablespoons margarine
1 tablespoon minced onion	paprika
1 tablespoon prepared horseradish	chopped parsley

Cook whole carrots in boiling, salted water until tender. Reserve 1/2 cup of cooking liquid and drain carrots. Cut carrots in smaller pieces and arrange in a shallow baking dish (8 or 9 inch square).

Combine the cooking liquid with mayonnaise, onion, horseradish, and salt. This much can be done ahead of time. Just before mealtime, pour sauce over carrots and sprinkle with cracker crumbs. Dot with margarine and sprinkle paprika and parsley over top. Bake, uncovered, in 375°F oven for 20 minutes.

Pat Jones   **Norwalk High School, Norwalk**

Pan De Elote

1 can (1 lb.) cream style corn
1 cup biscuit mix
1 egg, beaten
1 tablespoons butter, melted

½ cup milk
1 tablespoon sugar
1 can (4 oz.) green chiles
1 lb. jack cheese, shredded

Mix all but cheese and chiles and turn ½ the batter into a greased casserole. Cover with the chiles and ½ the cheese. Pour in the rest of the batter.

Bake at 400°F for 35 minutes. Put the last half of the cheese on top and bake 10 more minutes.

This is a nice change from potatoes or rice with a meal.

Anne Dahl   *Ensign Middle School, Newport Beach*

Lu's Mexicali Corn Casserole

Serves 12

2 cans (16 oz.) corn, drained
½ cup margarine, melted
2 eggs
2½ cups (10 oz.) cheddar cheese,
    shredded

1 cup sour cream
½ cup cornmeal
1 teaspoon salt
¼ teaspoon pepper
4 oz. green chiles, diced

Preheat oven at 350°F. Generously grease an 8 inch square casserole dish. In blender or food processor, puree 1 cup corn, margarine and eggs. Set aside. In large bowl, mix remaining corn, 2 cups cheese, sour cream, cornmeal, salt pepper and chiles. Add pureed mixture. Blend well. Pour into greased dish. Bake at 350°F for 50 minutes or until center is set. Top with remaining cheese. Bake 5 minutes longer or until cheese is melted.

Very light and tasty.

Lois Armstrong   *Sonora High School, La Habra*

Vegetable Kabobs

Serves 4 or 5

2 medium zucchini
2 yellow squash
8 medium sized fresh mushrooms
½ cup La Victoria Red Taco Sauce

1 tablespoon cilantro or parsley,
    chopped
4 to 5 cherry tomatoes

Cut zucchini and yellow squash into ½ inch chunks; steam over boiling water for 2 minutes.

Skewer zucchini and squash chunks, alternating with mushrooms, on 4 or 5 skewers. Stir together the Taco Sauce and cilantro; brush over vegetables.

Broil or grill for 4 minutes, brushing several times with sauce. Add a tomato onto each skewer; broil 2 minutes more. Serve with meats, poultry, or fish dishes.

La Victoria Foods, Inc.   *City of Industry*

Corn-Chile Rellenos

Serves 8 to 10

1 can (1 lb.) green chiles, whole	½ cup evaporated milk
1 lb. jack cheese, cut in strips	1 can cream style corn
1 lb. cheddar cheese, cut in strips	1 can whole kernel corn, drained
2 eggs	salt and pepper to taste

Remove seeds from chiles. Rinse. Fill chiles with both types of cheese. Place in a 9 x 13 inch baking dish. In a large bowl, mix eggs, evaporated milk, creamed corn, drained corn and seasonings. Pour over stuffed chiles. Bake at 350°F for 40 minutes.

Susan Roa Hope   *Lompoc Valley Middle School, Lompoc*

Papas y Zanahorias

Serves 4 to 6

1 pound carrots	2 tablespoons oil
2 pounds new potatoes	2 tablespoons water

Scrub and slice carrots and potatoes. Heat oil and water in skillet. Add sliced potatoes and carrots. Cover and simmer until vegetables are fork tender. Serve as a side dish.

Delicious with Biftec Enrollados.

Jeannie Burns   *Los Osos Junior High School, Los Osos*

Spanish Rice

Seves 4 to 6

1 cup rice	2½ cups chicken broth
¼ cup cooking oil	1 tablespoon parsley, chopped
1 small onion, chopped	1 jalapeno chile, minced
1 garlic clove, minced	1 teaspoon salt

Fry rice in hot oil with onion and garlic until lightly browned. Drain off oil. Add boiling broth, parsley, chile and salt. Cover tightly and simmer for 25 minutes without lifting the lid.

Amy Tavaglione   *Etiwanda High School, Etiwanda*

Spanish Rice

Serves 6 to 8

1 cup rice	1 clove fresh garlic
butter	1 fresh tomato
1 onion, chopped	½ teaspoon cumin
2 teaspoon salt	2 cups chicken broth

Brown the rice in a little bit of butter. Add remaining ingredients; cover and simmer until done and moisture is gone.

Green pepper can also be added.

Pat Jones   *Norwalk High School, Norwalk*

Mexican Rice

Serves 8 to 10

2 cups long grain rice
¼ cup oil
1 small onion, chopped
1 clove garlic

1 teaspoon salt
3 to 3¼ cups chicken broth
1 can (8 oz.) tomato sauce

Soak rice 15 minutes in hot water. Rub rice between hands until water is milky. Drain and rinse until water is nearly clear. Spread rice on towel covered tray to dry. Heat oil in a large heavy skillet. Add rice and saute until browned, stirring frequently. Chop onion, mash garlic with salt. Add onion and garlic paste to browned rice and saute until onion is tender. Add broth and tomato sauce. Stir. Cover and simmer over low heat until rice absorbs liquid and is tender and flaky (about 30 to 40 minutes).

Reiko Ikkanda   *South Pasadena High School, South Pasadena*

Mexican Fried Rice

Serves 4 to 6

1 cup long grain rice
1½ cups hot water
6 slices bacon, chopped
1 can condensed consomme
1 can (8 oz.) (1 cup) seasoned
   tomato sauce

¼ cup green pepper, chopped
¼ cup onion, chopped
1 clove garlic, minced
½ teaspoon cumin seed

Soak rice in hot water for 25 minutes; drain; let stand to dry, about 1 hour. Cook bacon until crisp; remove bacon. Add rice to drippings and cook until rice is lightly browned. Add bacon and remaining ingredients. Cover and cook over low heat, stirring occasionally, until rice is done and liquid is absorbed, about 30 minutes. (Add water during cooking if needed).

Excellent!

Brenda Burke   *Mt. Whitney High, Visalia*

Hot Mexican Rice Ring

Serves 8

1 teaspoon salt
1 teaspoon pepper
1 pint sour cream
¼ cup pimento, chopped

2 cups rice
1 cup monterey jack cheese,
   shredded
1 can (4 oz.) green chile peppers,
   chopped

Cook rice according to directions on package. Combine with remaining ingredients. Spoon into 8 cup ring mold, packing firmly. Bake in 350°F oven 30 minutes. Cool a few minutes, loosen around edges with a knife. Cover with plate. Carefully turn upside down and lift off mold. Garnish platter if desired with parsley and red and green chile peppers.

This is highly seasoned. For milder flavor, decrease amount of pepper and green chile peppers.

Pat Jones   *Norwalk High School, Norwalk*

Rice With Green Chiles

Serves 6 to 8

2½ cups water
1 cup raw rice
2 cups sour cream
salt to taste (optional)

½ lb. jack cheese
7 oz. green chiles, diced
3 tablespoons margarine or butter
¼ cup parmesan cheese

In a medium sized saucepan, bring the water to a boil. Add the rice, cover pan and simmer over low heat until the liquid is absorbed, approximately 20 to 25 minutes. Let the rice cool, Mix the cooked rice with sour cream and salt. Spread one-half the rice mixture in the bottom of a greased 1½ quart casserole. Sprinkle the jack cheese and green chiles on top and then add the rest of the rice. Dot with butter and sprinkle with the parmesan cheese. Bake uncovered at 350°F for 30 minutes.

I had this at a dinner served at Karen Roberts home. It is delicious.

Marianne Traw   **Ball Junior High School, Anaheim**

Vegetarian Tacos

Serves 6

1 cup bulgar wheat
2 cups hot water
2 green onions
2 tablespoons parsley
1 tomato
½ medium cucumber

½ medium green pepper
1 tablespoon soy sauce
2 cups cheddar cheese, grated
12 corn tortillas
garlic salt

Soak bulgar in 2 cups hot water until water is absorbed. Chop next 5 ingredients and add to bulgar. Toss bulgar and chopped veggies with soy sauce. Set aside. Spread cheese on the tortillas and sprinkle with garlic salt. Broil until cheese is melted. Fill center of tortillas with bulgar mixture, fold in half and eat. Messy? So what . . . enjoy!

An excellent low fat, semi low calorie, vegetarian substitute for tacos with meat!

Jennifer Jackson   **Corning High School, Corning**

Bean and Cheese Burritos

Serves 3 to 5

2 cups cooked pinto beans
   with some juice
   (canned or home-cooked)
2 tablespoons shortening
¼ teaspoon salt

1 teaspoon chili powder
¼ teaspoon cumin
1 tortilla per person
1 cup (about 4 oz.) cheddar
   cheese, grated

Put the beans in a large mixing bowl and mash them with the pastry blender. Melt the shortening in a large frying pan over low to medium heat. Spoon in the mashed beans, salt, chili powder and the cumin. Stir constantly. Cook over medium heat for 5 minutes. If they get a little dry, add a couple tablespoons of water. Equally divide the beans among the tortillas. Sprinkle on the cheese and roll up. Serve with salsa.

Kathy Williams   **Jurupa Junior High, Riverside**

Souffle Ole

Serves 2

1/2 cup ricotta cheese
1/3 cup Jack or Swiss cheese,
  shredded
2 tablespoons Romano or
  parmesan cheese, grated
3 eggs, separated
2 tablespoons any favorite
  La Victoria Salsa

1 to 2 tablespoons La Victoria
  Nacho Sliced Jalapenos
1 tablespoon cilantro or
  parsley, chopped
1 tablespoon water
1/8 ground cumin

Stir together the ricotta, Jack cheese, and grated Romano cheese. Stir in egg yolks; set aside. For filling, stir in the Salsa, Jalapenos, and cilantro. Set aside.

On high speed of electric mixer, beat egg whites with water and cumin till mixture forms stiff peaks. Fold 1/3 of the whites into the cheese mixture; fold in remaining whites. (Do not stir.) Spoon 1/2 of the souffle mixture into a 2 cup souffle dish (or two 1 cup dishes). Spoon filling mixture over; then top with remaining souffle mixture, spreading to cover filling.

Bake souffle in a 425°F oven for 10 to 15 minutes, or till souffles are puffed and golden brown. Serve immediately.

La Victoria Foods, Inc.   *City of Industry*

Mexican Pizza

Serves 4 (makes 1 12 inch pizza)

1 package active dry yeast
2/3 cup warm water
1/2 teaspoon sugar
1/8 teaspoon salt
1 1/2 tablespoons cooking oil

1 2/3 cup all purpose flour
3/4 cup tomato sauce
1/3 cup La Victoria Salsa Victoria,
  Salsa Suprema, or
  Green Chili Salsa

Desired toppings such as:
cheddar or jack cheese, shredded
ripe olives, sliced
green pepper strips

red pepper strips
green onions, sliced
guacamole for garnish

Additional La Victoria Salsa as needed

Dissolve yeast in warm water with sugar. Let stand to soften for 5 minutes. Stir in salt and oil. Stir in flour gradually, beating until smooth and elastic.

Knead dough 8 to 20 minutes. Place in a greased bowl; cover and let rise in a warm place till doubled (40 to 45 minutes).

Punch down dough; knead 10 times to remove any air bubbles. Line a 22 inch pizza pan with dough. Mix tomato sauce and salsa together; spread over dough. Sprinkle on desired toppings.

Bake in a 450°F oven for 15 to 18 minutes, or till crust is golden brown. Serve pizza garnished with guacamole. Pass with extra Salsa.

La Victoria Foods, Inc.   *City of Industry*

Green Enchiladas with Sauce

Serves 6

Filling

1/2 cup onion, chopped
1 tablespoon butter
2 cups cottage cheese
1 lb. white cheddar cheese,
  shredded
1/2 cup crushed (plain) tostados
  (Doritos)
2 tablespoons olives, chopped
2 tablespoons chiles, chopped
1 teaspoon salt
1 teaspoon MSG
12 tortillas (steam soft)

Sauce

1 can chicken broth
1 cup snipped parsley
2 tablespoons flour
1 can (2 oz.) Ortega chiles,
  chopped
2 cans cream of mushroom soup
1 large onion, finely diced
1 clove garlic, minced
1 teaspoon MSG
1/2 teaspoon salt

Cook onion in butter until tender. Add to cottage cheese, cheese, chips, olives, chiles, salt and MSG. Fill tortillas. Simmer chicken broth and parsley for 10 to 15 minutes. Thicken with 2 tablespoons flour, mixed with water. Add chiles, soup, onion, garlic, MSG and salt to chicken broth mixture. Spread sauce over enchiladas. Bake for 20 minutes at 350°F. Place sour cream on table for topping.

This dish always gets raves when I serve it.

Vicki Giannetti   Foothill High School, Sacramento

Green Enchiladas

Serves 4 to 6

12 corn tortillas
1/2 cup cooking oil
2 cups (8 oz.) monterey jack
  cheese, shredded
3/4 cup onion, chopped
1/4 cup butter or margarine
1/4 cup all purpose flour
2 cups chicken broth
1 cup sour cream

1 can (4 oz.) jalapeno peppers,
  seeded and chopped
1 medium tomato, finely chopped
1/2 cup onion, finely chopped
2 finely chopped jalapeno peppers
  with seeds, finely chopped
1/4 cup tomato juice
1/2 teaspoon teaspoon salt

In skillet, cook tortillas, one at a time, in hot oil for 15 seconds on each side. (Do not overcook or they won't roll. Place 2 tablespoons shredded cheese and 1 tablespoon chopped onion on each tortilla; roll up. Place seam side down, in an 11 x 7 x 1½ inch baking dish. In saucepan, melt butter or margarine; blend in flour. Add chicken broth all at once; cook and stir until mixture thickens and bubbles. Stir in sour cream and the 4 ounce can of peppers; heat through, but do not boil. Pour over tortillas in baking dish. Bake for 20 minutes at 425°F. Sprinkle remaining cheese on top; return to oven for 5 minutes or more until cheese melts.

Serve with **Spicy Pepper Sauce**: In mixing bowl, combine finely chopped tomato, ½ cups onion, remaining jalapeno peppers, tomato juice and ½ teaspoon salt.

Brenda Burke   Mt. Whitney High, Visalia

Vegetable Enchilada

Serves 4 to 6

6 cups assorted vegetables
zucchini, broccoli, carrots,
onions, etc.) cut into small pieces
2 tablespoons vegetable oil
⅛ teaspoon chili powder
⅛ teaspoon cumin

salt, pepper & other spices to taste
1 cup cheddar cheese, grated
1 cup jack cheese, grated
1 dozen flour tortillas
1 jar chile salsa

Cook vegetables in oil until crisp and tender. Add spices and half of each kind of cheese into pot. When cheese melts, fill tortilla with vegetable mixture and roll closed. Spoon salsa across top and sprinkle with rest of cheese. Bake at 350°F until hot.

EVEN the KIDS like this one and it's a good way to get your vegetables.

Ruth Whiteley   **Roosevelt Junior High School, Kingsburg**

Stacked Cheese Enchiladas

Serves 5 to 6

10 corn tortillas
salad oil, shortening or lard for
frying tortillas
2 cup red Ortega chile sauce
1 cup sharp cheddar cheese,
shredded
1 to 1½ cups green onions, chopped

Topping:

2 cups sour cream
1 cup onion, chopped
½ teaspoon cumin
1 cup longhorn cheese,
shredded

Fry tortillas in oil and dip in heated sauce. Place one tortilla in a small shallow ungreased casserole. Sprinkle 1 or 2 tablespoons cheese, 2 tablespoons onion, and a little of the remaining sauce over the surface of the tortilla. Add the remaining tortillas, preparing each layer the same way. Pour remaining sauce over the stack and top with remaining cheese.

Prepare the topping by blending all ingredients together. Place topping on tortilla stack. Bake uncovered in 350°F oven for 15 to 20 minutes or until hot. Cut in wedges to serve.

Donna Lee   **Elsinore Junior High School, Lake Elsinore**

Sour Cream Enchiladas

Serves 6

12 corn tortillas
oil
2 cups cheese, grated
½ cup green onion, chopped

1 cup sour cream
1 can cream of chicken soup
4 oz. green chiles, diced
optional: ¼ cup olives, chopped

Heat tortilla shells in oil to just soften. Place between paper towels. Mix cheese and onion together and roll up inside tortillas. Place filled tortillas in oiled baking pan.

Mix together sour cream, soup and chiles (olives if using). Pour over tortillas. Bake at 350°F for 25 minutes. More cheese may be placed over sour cream mixture before baking if desired.

Bonnie Parks   **Big Pine High School, Big Pine**

Chile Rellenos with Salsa

Serves 4

8 Anaheim chiles (use fresh
   California green chiles, peeled
   or canned Ortega whole ones)
½ lb. monterey jack cheese,
   cut into 8 long strips

4 eggs, separated
¾ cup flour
1 tablespoon water
½ teaspoon salt
cooking oil

If you use canned chiles, drain them and remove seeds (take seeds out through top or make a slight slit on side). Place a slice of cheese about ½ inch wide, ½ inch thick and one inch shorter than the chile inside of each chile. Beat 4 egg whites until they form soft peaks, put aside. Beat yolks with 1 tablespoon water and ¼ cup all purpose flour and ½ teaspoon salt until they are thick and creamy; fold yolk mixture carefully into egg whites, being careful not to knock the air out of the egg white mixture. Put about ½ cup flour on a dinner plate. Dip the stuffed chile in the flour mixture on both sides, then dip the stuffed chile into the fluffy batter. Heat about 1½ inch of salad oil in an electric skillet over medium to medium-high temperature. Place the batter coated chiles in the hot oil. When the bottoms are a golden brown, gently turn using a spatula and a fork and cook the other side (it takes about 3 to 4 minutes per side). Drain on a paper towel. The rellenos taste especially good with a good salsa, such as Salsa de Jitomate served on top or alongside.

Salsa de Jitomate:

¼ cup onion, finely chopped
1 clove garlic, minced
1 tablespoon butter
1 can (15 oz.) tomato sauce
   (Spanish style if possible)

⅓ cup water
¼ teaspoon salt
¼ teaspoon oregano leaves

Saute onion and garlic in butter until translucent. Add tomato sauce, water, salt and oregano leaves. Simmer uncovered for 8 to 12 minutes. Makes two cups.

Chiles rellenos are very popular foods in most authentic Mexican restaurants. Usually they are stuffed with cheese (jack or cheddar) but they may also be stuffed with a spicy hamburger mixture; usually called "Chiles Rellenos Con Picadillo". Most students reject the idea of cooking "chiles" because they think they'll be too hot, but once they've prepared them, they usually dash home and make them for their families.

Carole Jackson   **Apple Valley High School, Apple Valley**

Chile Rellenos

Serves 8

8 green peppers
1 can (16 oz.) tomatoes
1 small onion, cut up
1 teaspoon beef bouillon granules
dash pepper
dash ground cinnamon
4 cups monterey jack or cheddar
   cheese, or 1 lb. (or 4 cups)
   Picadillo, heated

8 egg yolks
2 tablespoons water
1/4 cup all purpose flour
1/2 teaspoon salt
8 egg whites
fat for frying
cilantro or parsley

Broil peppers 2 inches from heat for about 15 minutes, turning often, until all sides are blistered. Place peppers in a paper or plastic bag. Close bag and let stand 20 minutes or until cool enough to handle.

Meanwhile, make tomato sauce. In blender container combine tomatoes, onion, bouillon granules, pepper and cinnamon. Cover and keep warm over low heat while preparing peppers. Peel peppers; remove stems and seeds. Stuff each pepper with 1/2 cup of the cheese or hot Picadillo. Set aside. Slightly beat egg yolks and water. Add flour and salt; beat 6 minutes or until thick and lemon-colored. Beat egg whites until stiff peaks form. Fold in egg yolks into whites.

In a large skillet, heat 1/2 inch fat to 375°F. For each serving, spoon about 1/3 cup egg batter into fat, spreading batter in a circle. Fry 3 to 4 at a time. As batter begins to set, gently top each mound with stuffed chile. Cover with another 1/3 cup batter. Continue cooking 2 to 3 minutes more, until underside is brown. Turn carefully; brown second side. Drain on paper toweling; keep warm in 300°F oven while preparing remainder. Serve with tomato sauce; garnish with snipped cilantro or parsley.

Claudia L. Henry   *Colfax High School, Colfax*

Quick Spanish Omelette

Serves 1

2 eggs, beaten
1 tablespoon water
dash salt
1 tablespoon butter or margarine

1/2 cup cheddar or monterey jack
   cheese, shredded
1/2 cup La Victoria Green Chili
   Sauce

Cooking time: 5 minutes.

Beat eggs with fork till frothy; add water and salt and beat again. Melt the butter in a 10 inch skillet; pour in eggs. Tilt pan to distribute egg mixture evenly; cover and cook over medium heat till eggs are set and bottom is lightly browned.

Sprinkle with cheese; fold omelette in half. Heat Green Chili Sauce in small saucepan and pour over omelette. Cover till cheese is soft; turn onto plate. Serve.

La Victoria Foods, Inc.   *City of Industry*

Spanish Omelette

Serves 2

4 eggs
¼ cup water
½ teaspoon salt
pinch of pepper

1 tablespoon butter
½ cup cheese, shredded
¾ cup sauce (see recipe below)

Mix eggs, water, salt and pepper with fork. Heat butter in a 10 inch omelette pan or skillet until just hot enough to sizzle a drop of water. Pour in egg mixture. Mixture should set at edges at once. With pancake turner, carefully draw cooked portions at edges toward center, so uncooked portions flow to bottom. Tilt skillet as it is necessary to hasten flow of uncooked eggs. Slide pan rapidly back and forth over heat to keep mixture in motion and sliding freely.

Spread ½ of the sauce (recipe below) down the center of the omelette. Sprinkle with ¼ cup cheese, with pancake turner fold in half or roll, turning out onto platter with a quick flip of the wrist. Spread remaining sauce over the top. Sprinkle with remaining ¼ cup cheese.

Sauce

1 tablespoons butter
3 tablespoons green pepper or
  celery, chopped
2 tablespoons onion, chopped

1 tomato, chopped
4 oz. tomato sauce
1 tablespoon salsa

Melt butter in a small saucepan. Saute chopped vegetables until tender. Add tomato sauce and salsa. Cook over low heat 8 to 10 minutes. Makes approximately ¾ cup sauce.

Sydney Fox   *Orange Glen High School, Escondido*

Huevos Rancheros

Yields 12

1 to 2 cloves garlic, minced
1 tablespoon oil
1 can (16 oz.) stewed tomatoes
1 can (12 oz.) Ortega green chile
  salsa
2 cups cheddar cheese, grated
2 cups jack cheese, grated
1 can (28 oz.) refried beans

1 to 2 avocados, for garnish
1 dozen corn tortillas
oil for frying tortillas
1 dozen eggs
1 teaspoon water
margarine for frying eggs
1 pint sour cream

In medium saucepan, saute minced garlic in 1 tablespoon oil. Puree tomatoes in blender or mash if you do not like big chunks. When garlic is clear, add green chile salsa and stewed tomatoes. Simmer on low heat. Grate cheese, heat beans, peel and slice avocado. Fry 1 tortilla at a time in 2 tablespoons oil in a small frying pan on high heat. Turn tortilla once, remove and drain. Beat 1 egg with 1 teaspoon water in a small bowl. Fry in 1 tablespoon butter in small frying pan, turning once. Remove and assemble as follows on a dinner plate: tortilla, beans, egg, sauce, cheese, dollop of sour cream, sliced olives and avocado slices.

A speedy, but delicious brunch idea.

Patricia Dyle   *Kennedy High School, La Palma*

Mexican Quiche ⓜ

Serves 4

4 flour tortillas, 6 inch size
4 oz. jack cheese with peppers,
  sliced
1 can (3 oz.) French fried onions
  (1²/₃ cups)

2 cups milk
4 eggs, beaten
¹/₂ teaspoon salt
¹/₂ teaspoon chili powder
¹/₄ teaspoon dry mustard

Gently press a tortilla in each of 4 individual casserole dishes; top with cheese slices and ¾ (1¼ cups) onion rings. In a saucepan, heat milk almost to boiling. Gradually add to eggs; stir in salt, chili powder and mustard. Divide egg mixture evenly between casseroles. Bake at 350°F for 23 minutes. Sprinkle with rest of onions and bake 5 minutes more, until knife inserted comes out clean. Let stand 5 minutes.

To microwave: cook uncovered 6 minutes turning and rearranging three times. Sprinkle reserved onions on top. Let stand 10 minutes.

Jan McKinnon   *Dexter Junior High School, Whittier*

Quiche Mexicana

Makes 4 individual quiches

2¹/₂ cups Monterey jack cheese,
  grated
6 eggs, well beaten
¹/₂ cup half and half
¹/₃ cup onion, finely chopped
1 can (4 oz.) green chiles, diced
1 jar (2 oz.) pimentos, diced

¹/₄ teaspoon Lawry's Seasoned Salt
¹/₈ teaspoon Lawry's Garlic Powder
  with Parsley
Lawry's Seasoned Pepper, to taste
4 (8 inch) flour tortillas
vegetable oil

Combine all ingredients, except tortillas and oil, in a large bowl; mix thoroughly and set aside. Brush tortillas lightly with oil and place in small souffle or custard cups, to form tortilla quiche cups. Pour about ¾ cup of egg mixture into each quiche cup. Bake in 325°F oven for 20 to 30 minutes.

Barbara Boling   *Orange High School, Orange*

Breakfast Quesadillas

Serves 2

1 large flour tortilla, warmed
2 tablespoons cheddar or jack cheese, shredded
2 tablespoons La Victoria Salsa Suprema
Fillings: Use 2 to 3 tablespoons of the following:
green onion, sliced
red onion, chopped
avocado, diced
bacon, cooked and crumbled
sausage or ham or cooked
  poultry or beef, shredded
3 to 4 slices La Victoria Nacho Sliced Jalapenos

Open warm tortilla onto a baking sheet. Sprinkle half the tortilla with the cheese, salsa, and fillings. Top with jalapeno slices. Fold over top half of tortilla; moisten all inside edges with a few drops of water and fold edges over. Press together. Bake in a 450°F for 5 minutes. To serve, cut into wedges or strips. Serve hot.

La Victoria Foods, Inc.   *City of Industry*

Mexican Crepes

½ lb. ground beef
2 tablespoons shortening
¼ cup onion, finely chopped
¼ cup green pepper, finely chopped
¼ cup celery, finely chopped
¼ cup mushrooms, finely chopped
¼ cup stuffed green olives

1 teaspoon curry powder or
   chili powder
½ teaspoon salt
⅛ teaspoon pepper
1 can (6 oz.) tomato paste
¾ cup water
parmesan cheese

Saute ground beef and vegetables in 2 tablespoons shortening. Add seasonings, tomato paste and water. Simmer 15 minutes. Divide evenly into 10 crepes. Sprinkle with parmesan cheese. Place in 400°F oven for 3 to 5 minutes until lightly brown.

Barabara Boling   *Orange High School, Orange*

Mexican Cheese Puffs

Serves 3 (2 tortillas each)

1 cup sour cream
1 can (4 oz.) green chiles, diced
bottled hot chili sauce

1 lb. monterey jack cheese
6 flour tortillas
salad oil

Mix sour cream with ¼ cup diced chiles, about ½ can. Add a few drops of hot sauce. Chill. Slice cheese ¼ inch thick. To warm tortillas, place one at a time on oven rack in 350°F oven for 15 to 30 seconds. Put about ⅙ of cheese in center of warmed tortilla and sprinkle with some of the remaining diced chiles. Sprinkle with hot sauce to taste. Fold in two opposite sides and roll tortilla around filling, enclosing cheese completely. Fasten with picks. When all are filled, cover with damp paper towels until ready to cook. Heat ½ inch salad oil in a 10 inch skillet until it sizzles when corner of tortilla is dipped into it. Put 3 tortilla rolls in hot oil and cook 5 mintues, turning once. Drain on paper towels. Repeat with remaining rolls. Remove picks and serve hot with chilled sour cream.

Rather like a Mexican version of a hot cheese sandwich. To make the menu a little more filling, serve with rice.

Pat Jones   *Norwalk High School, Norwalk*

Nancy's Mexican Platter

Serves 6

1 large can refried beans
1 medium can green chiles
1 medium can tomatoes, chopped
½ lb. cheddar cheese

1 small can black olives, sliced
1 small sour cream
mashed avocado
corn chips

Spread large round pizza pan with beans. Layer chiles, tomatoes, cheese and olives in smaller circles so a row of each shows. Heat ingredients 1 through 5 for 10 to 15 minutes at 325°F or until cheese melts. Top with sour cream and avocado. Serve with Dorito or other corn chips around outer edge of pan. Stand them up in the beans. Also extra chips in a basket nearby.

Nancy Hobberlin   *Arroyo Grande High School, Arroyo Grande*

Beef & Pork Entrees

Mexican Beefies Ⓜ

Serves at least 10

5 lbs. chuck roast
  (7 bone, or blade)
3 tablespoons fat from drippings
2 large onions, chopped
1 can (4 oz.) green chiles, diced
1 cans (7 oz. each) chile salsa

¼ teaspoon garlic powder
4 tablespoons flour
2 teaspoons salt
1 teaspoon ground cumin
flour tortillas

Garnish:

lettuce
tomatoes
black olives

guacamole
sour cream
picante sauce

5 lb. chuck roast, roasted in a 200°F oven covered and no seasonings for 12 hours. Cool and save drippings. Shred roast into small pieces, set aside. In a large frying pan, put 3 tablespoons fat, add chopped onions, saute until clear. Add green chiles, chile salsa, garlic powder, flour, salt and ground cumin. Cook for one minute. Add reserved meat juices and shredded meat, heat through. At this point, you have a basic meat mixture. You can refrigerate or freeze or continue ahead for Mexican beefies.

Put enough oil to cover the bottom of a frying pan ¼ inch deep. Heat to medium heat. Put ¼ to ½ cup meat mixture in middle of a tortilla. Fold up to make a rectangle. Fry until golden brown on both sides. Place on bed of shredded lettuce, garnish with tomatoes, olives, guacamole, sour cream. Serve with picante sauce.

To reduce calories, instead of frying meat filled tortilla, pop them into the microwave for about 45 seconds to soften and heat tortilla.

This recipe was originally developed by the Siskiyou County Cowbelles — and teenagers love them.

Merlina Phillips   **McCloud High School, McCloud**

Flautas

Serves 6

2 lbs. ground beef or shredded
  roast beef
3 tablespoons chili powder
salt
pepper
1 tablespoon ground cumin
2 tablespoons flour

20 6 inch flour tortillas
water
lettuce, chopped
tomatoes, chopped
cheddar cheese, grated
guacamole
sour cream

In a skillet, over medium heat, saute beef until lightly brown. Drain fat. Add chili powder, salt, pepper and cumin. Mix well. Sprinkle flour over meat. When flour is absorbed and none can be seen, add enough water to moisten mixture. Simmer for 5 minutes. Stir occasionally and keep warm.. Heat tortillas in warm, ungreased frying pan for 30 seconds on each side, turning only once. Place 3 to 4 tablespoons of meat mixture across center of each tortilla. Cover with lettuce, tomatoes and cheese. Roll up. Top with guacamole and dabs of sour cream. Serve at once.

Jan Oliver   **Irvine High School, Irvine**

Chimichanga

Serves 8 to 12

2 lbs. flank steak,
  cut in 1½ inch cubes
¾ cup bell pepper, diced
½ cup onion, diced
5 tomatillos, diced
4 medium ripe tomateos, chopped
oil

½ teaspoon ground cumin
3 cloves garlic, diced
2 teaspoons bland chili powder
5 cups beef broth from flank steak
1½ teaspoons salt
1 teaspoon oregano leaves
tortillas (11 inch)

Boil the flank for 1½ hours, then shred. Saute bell peppers, onions, tomatillos and tomatos in 2 tablespoons of oil. Simmer the cumin, garlic, chili
powder, beef broth, salt and oregano for 10 minutes. Add the shredded
steak and sauteed mixture and bring to a second boil. Warm 11 inch
tortillas to soften. Add about ½ cup of the meat mixture to each and fold
envelope style, with sides folded in. Secure with toothpicks and drop into
350°F oil until golden brown.

Top with shredded lettuce, tomatoes, sour cream and guacamole. Garnish
with olives, green onion and radish flowers.

Sydney Fox   *Orange Glen High School, Escondido*

Steak Tacos with Guacamole (Beef Strip Tacos)

Yields 8

8 packaged taco shells
1 lb. top round or sirloin steak,
  cut ¾ inch thick
2 tablespoons salad oil or olive oil
1 medium sized onion,
  finely chopped
1 clove garlic, minced
⅛ teaspoon ground cumin

½ teaspoon salt
3 tablespoons canned tomato
  sauce
2 tablespoons raisins
1½ cups lettuce, shredded
1½ cups cheddar or jack cheese,
  shredded
guacamole (recipe follows)

Place taco shells on a pie pan; cover with foil and heat in a 350°F oven for
10 minutes. Slice meat across the grain into ¾ inch wide strips. Heat 1
tablespoon oil in a large frying pan; add onion, and saute over medium heat
until golden. Remove from pan and set aside. Add remaining 1 tablespoon
oil to pan and saute meat over medium high heat, stirring until it loses its
pink color. Add garlic, cumin, salt, tomato sauce, raisins, and sauteed
onion and simmer 2 minutes for flavors to blend. Spoon meat sauce into hot
taco shells, arrange on a platter, and pass bowls of lettuce, cheese, and
guacamole to spoon over.

Guacamole

1 large avocado, mashed
3 tablespoons canned green
  chile salsa

2 tablespoons lemon juice
2 tablespoons sour cream
2 tablespoons mayonnaise
¼ teaspoon salt

Mix ingredients together in order listed.

Sydney Fox   *Orange Glen High School, Escondido*

Mexicali Vegetable Soup, page 34

Breakfast Quesadillas, page 54

Prawns with Salsa, Main Dish, page 96

La Victoria's Taco Salad, page 26

Flat Tacos

Serves 4 to 6

2 lb. ground beef
1/2 cup onion, chopped
salt, to taste
pepper, to taste
1 can (16 oz.) tomato sauce
1 can (10 oz.) red chile sauce
12 corn tortillas
oil for shallow frying

1 lb. cheddar cheese, grated
1 head lettuce, chopped
optional servings:
  olives
  tomato wedges
  green onions, chopped
  sour cream

Brown ground beef and onion. Season with salt and pepper. Combine tomato sauce and chile sauce in pan large enough for dipping tortillas. Heat the sauces to a simmer. Add about 1/2 cup of the sauce mixture to the meat and mix well. Lightly fry the tortillas in a small amount of oil, one at a time.

To "build" tacos, dip a fried tortilla into the tomato sauce and put it on a plate. Add a layer of the meat, then a layer of grated cheese, then repeat. Make as many layers as desired per serving. Keep them warm in the oven as you do the others. To serve, surround the taco stack with the lettuce and garnish with the olives, tomatoes or onions. Top with a dollop of sour cream.

This dish is not real spicy-hot. For those with spicier taste buds, you could use straight chile sauce, or "pass the hot sauce" at the table.

Donna Neel   **Dale Junior High School, Anaheim**

Fiesta Party Steak
(Mexican-style Steak)

Serves 6 to 8

1/2 cup flour and 1 teaspoon salt combined
2 lbs. round steak, pounded, cut in serving sized pieces, and dredged in flour mixture. Brown in small amount of oil over medium high heat. Reserve in large flat casserole baking dish.

Salsa: *(This can be made ahead and frozen successfully)*
Saute in 2 tablespoons oil:
  1 large clove garlic, minced and 1 cup onion, chopped.
Add:

1 can (4 oz.) mushrooms,
  including liquid
1 can (#2 1/2) tomatoes, cut up,
  including juice
1 teaspoon cumin (ground)
1 teaspoon chili powder

1 teaspoon salt
1 can (small size) Ortega chiles,
  diced
pepper to taste
1 1/2 cups jack cheese for garnish

Simmer about 45 minutes or until thickened. Taste and correct seasonings if necessary. Pour over browned steak pieces. Cover with foil. Bake at 325°F for 1 hour 45 minutes. Sprinkle with 1 1/2 cups grated jack cheese. Bake 15 minutes more, uncovered. If desired, assemble steak the day before and refrigerate before baking (add 20 minutes to baking time).

Good with refried beans, green salad, and fried tortilla chips or hot flour tortillas.

Linda Braxton   **Grace Davis High School, Modesto**

Carne Asada

Serves 3 to 4

1 flank steak *	1/2 teaspoon garlic powder
1/4 cup chili powder	1/2 teaspoon salt
1/2 cup oil	1/2 teaspoon MSG
1/3 cup lemon juice	1/2 teaspoon oregano

* May substitute other cuts of beef, pork, or chicken.
However, carne means beef.

Tenderize flank steak by pounding or cutting across grain diagonally. Mix all other ingredients to make a marinade. Marinate flank steak overnight or at least 12 hours. Grill on medium coals. It may also be broiled, steamed in its own juices or used for taco filling.

Serve with beans and flour tortillas for a truly Mexican meal. Preparation time is approximately 10 minutes. What a meal for so little time.

Dotti Jones   *Etiwanda High School, Etiwanda*

Mexican Pepper Steak

Serves 6

1/4 cup butter or oil	1/2 lb. fresh mushrooms or
3 medium steaks	2 cans mushrooms
6 green onions, cut in rings	1/2 cup white wine
1/2 cup parsley	salt and pepper
	lemon and tomato slices to garnish

Put oil or butter in frying pan, heat. Fry steaks quickly and remove to hot platter. In remaining oil, add onions, parsley, mushrooms, wine, salt and pepper and cook until mushrooms are tender. Pour over the steaks. Decorate the platter with lemon and tomato slices.

Antoinette De Neve   *Jones Junior High, Baldwin Park*

Beefsteak Mexican Style

Serves 6

2 1/2 lbs. round steak	1 1/2 cups water
2 to 4 teaspoon oil or shortening	1 or 2 La Victoria Whole Marinated
1 onion, sliced	Jalapeno Peppers, rinsed
1 clove garlic, minced	and seeds removed
1 chorizo or Italian sausage,	12 small new potatoes, peeled
skinned and sliced	1/2 cup chopped fresh cilantro
1/4 to 1/2 cup La Victoria Salsa	or parsley
Casera (or preferred hotness)	

Cut round steak into serving size pieces. In a large skillet heat oil or shortening; brown meat pieces on all sides. Remove meat from pan. In same pan saute onion, garlic, and sausage; drain off excess fat. Return meat to pan; add Salsa and water. Rinse, remove seeds and chop Jalapeno Peppers; add to pan. Cover and simmer 1 1/2 hours. Add potatoes. Cover and simmer 25 minutes longer or till meat and potatoes are tender. Sprinkle with cilantro or parsley to serve.

La Victoria Foods, Inc.   *City of Industry*

Cuete Mechado

Serves 6

3 slices ham, ¼ inch thick (½ lb.)
1 carrot
2 garlic cloves
1 tablespoons white vinegar
1 teaspoon cumin
4 lb. rump roast
½ onion, diced

1 tablespoon cooking oil
1 can (6 oz.) tomato paste
1 bay leaf
½ teaspoon salt
½ teaspoon black pepper
½ teaspoon oregano

Cut ham and carrot into 1 inch strips. Put one clove garlic, diced, plus vinegar and cumin in small bowl. Make small incisions in the roast with a knife. Insert 1 strip ham and 1 piece carrot and a few pieces of garlic into incisions. Saute onion, and other diced garlic in oil in a dutch oven. Brown roast turning constantly for about 15 minutes; add tomato paste, bay leaf, cumin mixture, salt, pepper and oregano. Bring a boil; add 3½ cups water or until roast is covered. Boil for 5 minutes uncovered. Cover and simmer for one hour. Remove from broth. Slice roast.

Strain broth. Serve roast slices on lettuce leaves. Pour some broth over sliced meat.

The first time I had this recipe was when we visited at the home of an exchange student from Mexico.

Deanne Moody   **Monte Vista High School, Spring Valley**

Mexican Pot Roast

Serves 12

5 lbs. top round of beef
¼ cup cooking oil
3 cloves garlic, minced
1 large red onion, diced
3 stalks celery, sliced
3 carrots, peeled and sliced
2 cups La Victoria Salsa Victoria
   or Salsa Suprema

½ cup all purpose flour
1 cup La Victoria Chili Dip
2 cups beef stock
2 bay leaves
2 to 3 teaspoons crushed dried
   thyme or oregano leaves
   (optional)
¼ cup chopped parsley

Brown meat in hot oil on all sides; remove from pan. Saute the garlic, onion, celery, and carrots in oil about 5 minutes till tender.

Stir together the Salsa and flour; add to pan with Chili Dip. Blend well and cook for 2 or 3 minutes, stirring constantly.

Stir in the beef stock, seasonings, and parsley; bring mixture to boiling. Return meat to pan and cover. Place pan in a 350°F oven for about 1¾ hours or till meat is very tender. Cut meat into serving size portions; serve with sauce.

La Victoria Foods, Inc.   **City of Industry**

Lee's Rolled Tacos

Yields 3 dozen

1 medium size chuck roast
½ package dried Lipton Onion
   soup mix
2 onions, chopped

¼ cup water
3 dozen corn tortillas
oil
toothpicks

Line a roasting pan with a large piece of foil. Place the roast in the center of the foil. Put dried soup mix, chopped onions and water on top. Seal foil to make a tent around the roast. Bake at 325°F for 2½ hours. Let meat cool slightly. Shred meat to desired size.

Heat ¼ inch of oil in a skillet. Place each tortilla in hot oil for about 10 to 15 seconds on each side to soften it. Drain on a paper towel. Place about 2 tablespoons of meat mixture in the center of each tortilla. Roll tightly and fasten with a toothpick. Fry in oil at medium temperature, turning occasionally, until light brown. Do 5 or 6 at a time and drain on paper towels. May be kept warm in oven while frying the rest, but are also good cold. Serve with your favorite salsa.

Ginny Rocheleau   *Muirlands Junior High School, La Jolla*

Mexicali Meatballs

Serves 6

1½ lbs. ground beef
¼ cup rice
½ cup onion, chopped
1 teaspoon salt
½ teaspoon worcestershire sauce

dash pepper
1 can (12 oz.) V-8 juice
5 small zucchini (4 cups sliced)
¼ cup cheddar cheese, grated
1 cup (12 oz.) whole corn, drained

Combine beef, rice ¼ cup onion, and seasonings. Toss lightly. Form into 20 meatballs. Pour V-8 juice into large frying pan. Add meatballs, remaining onion, zucchini and cheese. Cover and simmer 30 to 40 minutes, turning meatballs occasionally. Add corn; continue cooking 5 minutes. If desired, remove cover for last few minutes to allow sauce to thicken.

Nancy Earnest   *Victor Valley High School, Victorville*

Meat Loaf Suprema

Serves 6

2 lbs. ground beef
2 carrots, peeled and grated
1 green onion, minced
1 teaspoon salt
1 egg, beaten

2 to 4 tablespoons La Victoria
   minced Whole Marinated
   Jalapeno Peppers, rinsed
   and seeds removed
½ cup to ¾ cup La Victoria
   Salsa Suprema

Combine all ingredients except Salsa. Mix lightly but thoroughly. Shape into a loaf and place on a greased baking pan or pack lightly but firmly into a 9 x 5 inch loaf pan. Bake in a 375°F oven for 1 hour. Spoon Salsa Suprema over meatloaf; slice and serve.

La Victoria Foods, Inc.   *City of Industry*

Meatballs – Mexican Style

Serves 4

Meatballs:

½ lb. ground beef
½ cup bread crumbs
2 tablespoons milk

1 tablespoons onion, diced finely
1 egg
¼ teaspoon salt

Sauce:

¼ cup olives, sliced
dash pepper
dash garlic salt
dash cayenne pepper
⅓ cup juice from tomatoes
3 oz. tomato paste

1 tablespoon butter
2 tablespoons green pepper,
    chopped
2 tablespoon onion, chopped
1 can (15 oz.) tomatoes,
    drained and save juice

Combine beef, crumbs, milk, onion, egg and salt. Mix thoroughly, but lightly. Shape into small balls 1 inch in diameter. Place in baking dish; brown at 375°F for 25 to 30 minutes.

Melt 1 tablespoon butter in a skillet. Add green pepper and onion. Cook until tender. Add tomatoes, olives, pepper, garlic salt and cayenne pepper. Mix together ⅓ cup tomato juice and tomato paste. Add meatballs to sauce; stir lightly to mix. Bring to boil over medium heat. Cover; reduce heat. Simmer 30 minutes. For main dish, double recipe, serve over hot rice or noodles.

Bonnie Pius   **Sanger High School, Sanger**

Stir Fry South of the Border

Serves 4

1 lb. beef round steak
1 cup chile salsa
¾ cup cold water
2 tablespoons parsley, snipped
2 teaspoons vinegar
¾ teaspoon cornstarch
½ teaspoon sugar
½ teaspoon ground cumin
4 teaspoons salt
¼ teaspoon pepper

⅛ teaspoon cinnamon
1 clove garlic, minced
1 tablespoon cooking oil
1 small onion, chopped
1 can (7 oz.) corn with peppers
1 package (8 oz.) tortilla chips
1 cup lettuce, shredded
½ cup cheese, shredded
hot chile peppers

Cut partially frozen beef into diagonal bite sized strips. Place in a small bowl and add next ten ingredients. Preheat wok; add oil. Stir fry garlic in hot oil for 15 seconds. Add onion and cook 2 minutes, until tender. Remove onion. Add half of the beef. Stir fry 2 to 3 minutes. Remove and do other half. Return to wok and push away from the center. Stir sauce and add to center of wok; add corn. Stir all together to coat with sauce. Cover and cook 1 minute.

Arrange chips on 4 dinner plates. Top with meat mixture, remaining salsa, lettuce and cheese. Garnish with hot peppers. Serve immediately.

It's okay to use chicken rather than beef for less calories and fat.

Audrey Brown   **Loara High School, Anaheim**

Fajitas

Serves 4

1 lb. skirt steak cut across grain in
   1/4 inch strips or 1 lb. boned and
   skinned chicken
2 tablespoons oil
2 tablespoons lemon juice
1 teaspoon garlic powder
1 teaspoon salt
1/2 teaspoon ground oregano
1/2 teaspoon pepper
1/8 teaspoon liquid smoke
3 tablespoons oil
1 cup green pepper strips
1 cup thin onion wedges
1 cup thin tomato wedges
1/2 cup milk chunky taco salsa
8 hot flour tortillas

In a bowl, combine first 8 ingredients. Cover and refrigerate 6 to 8 hours. Heat 3 tablespoons oil in a skillet until very hot. Saute meat until it begins to lose redness. Add peppers and onions. Cook 1 to 2 minutes. Add tomato and salsa. Simmer. Serve immediately.

Serve with side dishes of guacamole, cilantro, or other vegetables.

Bonnie Shrock　　　　　　　　　**Kearny High School, San Diego**

Chile Verde

Serves 8

2/3 cup olive oil
4 lbs. chuck, cut in 1/2 inch cubes
6 to 7 cups tomatoes, peeled and
   coarsely chopped
2 large onions, finely chopped
2 cloves garlic, minced
7 oz. green chiles, diced
2 teaspoons dried oregano leaves,
   crushed
1 teaspoon cumin
1 teaspoon salt
1/2 teaspoon freshly ground pepper
1/3 cup fresh lime juice
   (about 3 limes)

Heat olive oil in a heavy skillet over moderate heat. Brown the meat, a few pieces at a time. Place browned meat into a 5 quart dutch oven. Add the rest of the ingredients to the dutch oven, cover and simmer over low heat, until meat is tender. (Approximately 2 hours).

Serve with refried beans and hot, buttered tortillas.

Debbie Scribner　　　　　　**North Tahoe High School, Tahoe City**

Chile Colorado

Serves 4 to 6

3 cups stew meat, cubed
3 tablespoons oil
2 tablespoons flour
3 tablespoons chili powder
1 large onion, chopped
1 clove garlic, crushed
1/4 teaspoon ground comino
1 bay leaf
3 cups water
salt and pepper to taste

Brown meat in oil. Add flour and brown. Add next 4 ingredients. Cook until onion is tender. Add water. Bring to a fast boil. Reduce heat. Add bay leaf and simmer until meat is tender. Add salt and pepper to taste.

Serve with rice, beans and flour tortillas.

Bonnie Shrock　　　　　　　　　**Kearny High School, San Diego**

Chalupa

Serves 6 to 8

3 lbs. boneless pork loin roast
2 lbs. pinto beans, uncooked
2 cloves garlic, chopped
1 teaspoon oregano
2 tablespoons chili powder
1 small size can jalapeno peppers
1 teaspoon cumin

Garnish:
avocados, chopped
corn chips
onions, chopped
cheese, grated
tomatoes, chopped
jicama, chopped

Combine all ingredients in crockpot or slow cooker, cover with water. Cook on high setting 6 hours, adding more water whenever liquid is absorbed, until beans are soft. Serve as stew in bowls. Top with desired garnish.

This is an old family recipe from New Mexico.

Linda Hubbs   Lone Pine High School, Lone Pine

Kathie's Favorite Chili

Serves 6 to 8

2 lbs. lean ground beef
1 medium onion, finely chopped
1 can (8 oz.) tomato sauce
1 package chili seasoning
2 whole bay leaves

¼ teaspoon powdered cloves
2 cans (16 oz. each) pinto or
   kidney beans
1 cup tomato juice for thinner chili
salt and pepper to taste

Brown meat and onion. Drain off any excess liquid or fat. Add tomato sauce, chili seasoning, bay leaves, chili powder, and cloves. Simmer 1½ to 2 hours. Add tomato juice for thinner chili if desired. Add beans. Simmer an additional 15 minutes. Remove bay leaves. Salt and pepper to taste before serving.

This is better if made a day before and refrigerated overnight. Using the crockpot is also very convenient.

Kathie Baczynski   Mt. Carmel High School, San Diego

Lou's Mex Tex Chili

Serves 8 to 10 (depends upon their appetite!)

1 lb. pinto beans, cooked
1 to 2 teaspoons salt
2 cloves garlic, minced finely
1 large onion, chopped
2 lbs. ground chuck
1 large can Mexican style stewed
   tomatoes (S & W)

2 small cans tomato sauce
2 to 4 tablespoons ground chili
1 tablespoon chocolate chips
   (optional, but this adds a
   distinctive flavor)
salt to taste

Soak beans overnight. Cook beans in a crockpot or large pot until tender. Add 1 teaspoon salt or salt to taste. Drain beans. Saute minced garlic and onions in large fry pan or dutch oven. Add ground meat and brown. Add rest of ingredients, except beans, and simmer for 30 minutes. Add beans and simmer 10 more minutes. Chili is best if it is made a day ahead and is refrigerated overnight for flavors to blend in nicely!

Lou Helen Yergat   Mission Viejo High School, Mission Viejo

Corn Cups With Beef Chili

Corn Cup Dough

6 tablespoons butter, at room
  temperature
3 oz. cream cheese, at room temp.

1 cup all purpose flour
½ cup cornmeal
pinch of salt

Cream together the butter and cream cheese with a mixer. Combine the flour, cornmeal and salt. Add it a little at a time, to the butter mixture, stirring constantly until well incorporated. Knead it lightly with your hands. Divide the dough into 1 inch balls and press them into small muffin tins, using your thumbs to form cups inside the mold. The dough cups should be as even as possible and come up to the top of the tins. Bake for 20 minutes or until a golden brown. Fill with beef chili and serve.

Beef Chili

3 slices bacon
1 lb. beef, thinly sliced and slivered
1 onion, finely chopped
2 garlic cloves, minced

1 jalapeno pepper, thinly sliced
1 teaspoon cumin
2 tablespoons chili powder
1 can (1½ lb.) whole tomatoes

To make the chili, heat a pan over a medium high flame and saute the bacon for a few minutes, until some of the fat is rendered. Add the beef slivers and onion to the pan. Reduce the heat to medium low and saute for 5 minutes. Add the garlic, pepper, cumin, and chili powder. Cook until the jalapeno pepper is soft, about 15 minutes. Add the tomatoes and stir well and cook over low heat until the liquid has evaporated, about 1 hour. If necessary, add 1 to 2 tablespoons of cornmeal to thicken the mixture. No liquid should be left in the pan before filling the corn cups.

ALTERNATE FILLING OF CHILE PEPPERS AND CHEESE:

2 jalapeno peppers, seeded and chopped
1 fresh chile pepper, seeded and finely chopped
1 sweet red pepper, seeded and finely chopped
3 tablespoons olive oil
1 cup sharp cheddar or monterey jack cheese, grated
salt and freshly ground pepper to taste

Saute the peppers in olive oil until soft, 5 to 6 minutes. Mix with grated cheese, season and spoon into corn cups immediately.

Lynn Robertson   *Esparto High School, Esparto*

Enchiladas

Serves 12

1 lb. ground beef
1 tablespoon taco seasoning mix
2 dozen corn tortillas
oil

1 can red chile sauce (Old El Paso
  or Las Palmas)
1 lb. cheddar or jack cheese,
  grated
1 onion, chopped

Brown ground beef, drain. Add seasoning. Fry tortillas in oil until soft. Dip in heated red chile sauce. Fill each tortilla with beef, cheese, onion; roll and place seam side down in baking pan. Top with extra cheese. Bake for 20 to 30 minutes at 350°F.

Cooked chicken or turkey can be substituted in place of beef.

April Herman   *Townsend Junior High School, Chino*

Enchiladas

Yields 12

Sauce

¼ cup flour
¼ cup shortening
2 tablespoons chili powder
½ teaspoon oregano
½ teaspoon cumin

½ teaspoon garlic powder
½ teaspoon salt
2 cups water
1 can (8 oz.) tomato sauce
3 beef bouillon cubes

For the sauce, brown flour in a large skillet. Add shortening and seasonings, making a paste. Add water gradually then add tomato sauce and crumble in bouillon cubes. Place in heat and cook until thick, stirring constantly.

Enchiladas

1½ lbs. ground beef
1 medium onion, chopped
salt
pepper
½ cup oil

1 dozen corn tortillas
enchilada sauce
24 black olives, pitted
¾ lb. cheddar cheese, grated

For the enchiladas, crumble ground beef and cook until done. Add chopped onion and continue cooking until onions are done. Salt and pepper to taste. Place ½ cup oil in pan and heat. Heat the tortillas in fat, one by one. Dip the tortillas in the sauce. Add 2 or 3 tablespoons ground beef mixture to each tortilla and 2 olives to each and sprinkle with cheese.

Roll up and cover with remaining sauce. Sprinkle cheese over the rolled tortillas (enchiladas) that have have been placed in a baking dish. Place in a 350°F oven until warmed thoroughly.

Nancy Jordan   *Merced High Scool, Merced*

Beef Enchiladas

Yields 6 to 12 enchiladas

1½ lbs. ground beef
1 medium onion, chopped
1 teaspoon salt
⅛ teaspoon garlic powder
⅓ cup bottled or canned taco sauce
1 cup ripe olives, quartered

12 corn tortillas
salad oil for frying tortillas
2 cans (10 oz. each) enchilada
  sauce
3 cups cheddar cheese, shredded
ripe olives, sliced & pitted for garnish

Crumble ground beef and saute with onions. Drain. Stir in salt, garlic powder, taco sauce and olives. Heat until bubbly. Dip tortillas, one at a time, in hot oil to soften; drain quickly. Heat enchilada sauce. Pour about ½ into an ungreased, shallow 3 quart baking dish. Place about ⅓ cup of the ground beef filling on each tortilla and roll to enclose filling. Place, flap side down, in the sauce in the bottom of the baking dish. Pour remaining enchilada sauce evenly over tortillas; cover with cheese. Bake uncovered in 350°F oven for about 15 to 20 minutes, or until heated thoroughly.

This recipe can be frozen or refrigerated (1 day), if taken directly from the refrigerator and baking time is increased to 45 minutes.

Garnish with olive slices. Serve with sour cream and green chile sauce.

Donna Goble   *Almondale School, Littlerock*

California Beef Enchiladas

Serves 8 to 10

Sauce:

3 tablespoons olive oil
1 clove garlic
¼ cup onion, chopped
2 tablespoons flour
1 can (29 oz.) tomato puree
1 tablespoon vinegar

1 beef bouillon cube
1 cup boiling water
3 tablespoons green chiles,
  chopped
½ teaspoon salt
dash pepper

Sauce: Mix all the sauce ingredients in a saucepan. Bring to a boil and simmer for 5 minutes. Set aside.

Filling Mixture:

1½ lbs. ground beef
1 clove garlic
1 or 2 tablespoons salt
1 tablespoon vinegar
1 tablespoon water

1 tablespoon chili powder
1 can kidney beans

1 dozen flour tortillas
½ lb. cheddar cheese, grated

Filling mixture: Brown the meat and garlic. Drain off the fat. Add the remaining filling ingredients. Set aside.

To assemble the enchiladas: Place ⅓ cup meat filling in each tortilla. Roll up the tortillas and place them in a greased 9 x 13 inch casserole. Pour sauce over the enchiladas. Sprinkle the casserole with grated cheese. Bake at 350°F for 25 to 30 minutes.

This casserole can be prepared ahead of time and reheated at the last minute! Serve with a salad for a delicious meal!

Bonnie Landin   **Garden Grove High School, Garden Grove**

Enchiladas

Serves 6

Sauce:

2 cans (8 oz.) tomato sauce
1 can (6 oz.) tomato paste
1 can tomato soup
½ teaspoon garlic powder
2 cups water
½ cup cooking oil
2 tablespoons chili powder
½ teaspoon salt

Filling:

1 lb. ground beef
1 cup onion, chopped
½ teaspoon salt
½ lb. cheddar cheese
1 can ripe olives, sliced
1 dozen tortillas (flour or corn)
cheddar cheese

Mix all sauce ingredients together and simmer 20 mintues. Brown beef. Add onions, salt, cheese and olives and mix together. Dip a tortilla into sauce and lay on a plate. Put ½ of mixture in center of tortilla and roll up. Repeat for all 12 tortillas. Place tortilla rolls in a 9 x 13 inch baking dish. Pour 1 cup of sauce over all. Bake for 20 minutes at 350°F, and sprinkle more cheese on top of enchiladas. Serve with remaining enchilada sauce.

Verna M. Buerge   **Turlock High School, Turlock**

Enchiladas

Serves 12

2 to 3 lbs. ground sirloin meat
salt and pepper to taste
2 medium onions, diced
3 cans (7 oz. each) Ortega green
  chile salsa
2 to 3 ripe avocados, thinly sliced

2½ or more lbs. monterey jack
  cheese
12 large flour tortillas
2 cans (7 oz. each) Ortega green
  chiles
12 oz. sour cream
pitted black olives

Fry meat in a frying pan. Drain grease off, season with salt and pepper. In the same pan, fry 2 medium onions, that have been diced into small pieces. Add to beef. Add some canned chile salsa to taste; mix well. Set aside. Slice avocados into fairly thin slices. Set aside. Grate all of the cheese. Set aside.

Line a very large (15½ x 10 x 2 inch) baking pan with foil. Grease lightly with Pam spray or an oil. Begin to assemble enchiladas: take one tortilla, layer first with the meat mixture, then avocado slices, then the jack cheese and 2 narrow strips of canned chile peppers that have been seeded. Adjust peppers according to taste for each enchilada. Lay each enchilada, seam side down, in pan. When done assembling the enchiladas, cover with the rest of the grated cheese and bake, covered, for 30 minutes or until hot, at 350°F. To serve, top with sour cream and some salsa sauce and decorate with some pitted black olives.

Everyone loves these! They are nice served with a Mexican rice dish and refried beans.

Nancy E. Smith   **Dale Junior High School, Anaheim**

Beef Enchiladas

Serves 18 to 20

3 lbs. beef stew meat
3 tablespoons salad oil or lard
3 small onions
3 cloves garlic, minced
3 teaspoons salt
¾ teaspoon pepper
3 teaspoons oregano
2 taplespoons chili powder

3 cups water
3 cans (8 oz. each) tomato sauce
36 corn tortillas
6 cans (10 oz.) Mexican red chile
  sauce
3 cups cheddar cheese, shredded
1½ cups onion, chopped (1 onion)
1 can ripe olives

Brown beef in oil. Add onion and garlic and seasonings; cook until soft. Add water, cover and simmer slowly 40 minutes. Shred beef (two forks work well). Add tomato sauce and simmer, uncovered until thick (about 15 minutes). Fry each tortilla briefly in hot oil to soften. Dip into heated chile sauce. Fill each tortilla with meat, chopped onion and shredded cheese, roll, place flap down in shallow casserole. When all are prepared, spoon remaining sauce over enchiladas, sprinkle with cheese. Garnish with olives. Heat at 350°F for 20 minutes.

May be prepared ahead of time.

Vicki Warner-Huggins   **Placer High School, Auburn**

Sour Cream Enchiladas

Serves 6

1 can (10 oz.) enchilada sauce
1 can (16 oz.) whole tomatoes,
  undrained and chopped
vegetable oil for frying
12 corn tortillas

3 cups Mexican Meat Mix, thawed
  (recipe follows)
1½ cups cheddar cheese, grated
1½ cups sour cream

Combine enchilada sauce and chopped tomatoes in a medium saucepan. Cook over medium heat until mixture boils. Reduce heat and simmer. Heat oil over medium high heat in a small skillet. Dip one tortilla at a time in hot oil for several seconds. Then dip in hot enchilada sauce mixture. Set aside. Heat Mexican meat in a small saucepan. Place ¼ cup Mexican meat on each tortilla and sprinkle with 2 tablespoons grated cheese. Roll up and place close together in a shallow casserole dish, seam side down. Pour remaining sauce over enchiladas. Sprinkle with additional grated cheese. Bake about 15 minutes and spoon sour cream over enchiladas and serve hot.

Wilma Reaser   *Hemet Junior High School, Hemet*

Mexican Meat Mix

Makes 3 one quart freezer containers

5 lbs. beef roast or part pork
3 tablespoons vegetable shortening
3 onions, chopped
1 can (4 oz.) chiles, chopped
2 cans (7 oz.) green chile salsa

¼ teaspoon garlic powder
4 tablespoons flour
salt to taste
1 teaspoon ground cumin
juice from beef roast

Cook roast until well done using a pressure cooker, cooking for 35 to 40 minutes and adding 1 cup water; or cook in oven at 200°F for 12 hours (no water). Drain meat, reserving juices; cool. Remove bones and shred meat. Melt shortening in a large skillet. Add onions and green chiles. Saute 1 minute and add chile salsa, garlic powder, flour, salt and cumin. Cook 1 minute over medium low heat. Stir in reserved meat juices and shredded meat. Cook 5 minutes until thick. Cool.

Put about 3 cups mix into three 1 quart freezer containers, leaving 1 inch space at the top. Seal and label containers. Freeze. Use within six months.

Use mix with green chile burritos, sour cream enchiladas, taco supreme, etc.

Wilma Reaser   *Hemet Junior High School, Hemet*

Chorizo

Yields 1 pound

1 lb. ground pork
1 teaspoon salt
2 tablespoons chili powder

1 garlic clove
1 teaspoon oregano
2 tablespoons vinegar

Mix all ingredients thoroughly. Crumble sausage in a skillet and cook thoroughly.

"May add beaten eggs to mixture and cook as scrambled eggs.

Bonnie Shrock   *Kearny High School, San Diego*

Sour Cream Enchiladas

Makes 1 dozen

1 dozen corn tortillas	1/4 cup butter
1/2 cup cooking oil	1/4 cup flour
2 cups jack cheese	2 cups chicken broth
3/4 cup onions, chopped	1 cup sour cream
1 lb. hamburger, browned	1 can (4 oz.) Ortega chiles, diced

Cook tortillas in hot oil, one at a time (approximately 15 seconds). Drain on paper towels. Mix together 1 cup of cheese with onion and meat. Place a scoop (1/2 of the mixture) on each shell. Roll up and place seam side down in a greased 9 x 13 inch pan.

To make sauce: melt butter, blend in flour. Add broth; stir until thick. Stir in sour cream and chiles. Pour sauce over enchiladas; top with cheese. Bake at 400°F for 20 minutes.

You can substitute 3 chicken breasts (cooked and diced) for the hamburger meat! They freeze great!

Kathy Crawford   *Thompson Junior High School, Bakersfield*

Picadillo (Mexican Hash)

Serves 4 to 10 depending on usage

1 lb. lean ground beef	pinch of ground cloves
1 onion, chopped	1/4 teaspoon ground cumin
3 tablespoons oil	1 teaspoon salt
1 cup solid pack tomatoes	1/2 cup raisins, plumped in 1/4 cup
2 tablespoons vinegar	hot stock or water
1 teaspoon sugar	1 can (4 oz.) peeled Ortega chiles
1 teaspoon cinnamon	1/2 cup blanched almonds, slivered

Brown meat and onion in oil. Add all other ingredients, except almonds, Stir to blend, bring to a boil; reduce heat and simmer 30 to 45 minutes. Stir in almonds. (Will freeze). Use as a filling for empanadas, tacos, enchiladas, tamales, etc.

This is a recipe from "Elena's Secrets of Mexican Cooking" by Elena Zelayeta.

Betsy Cosart   *Monache High School, Porterville*

Biftec Enrollados

Serves 4 to 6

1 lb. bacon	2 tablespoons oil
round steak	

Sauce:

1 large onion, sliced	1/4 teaspoon cinnamon
1 garlic clove	1/2 teaspoon sugar
1/2 teaspoon salt	1 lb. canned whole tomatoes
4 whole cloves	cilantro

Cook bacon until soft. Slice round steak into 1/2 inch slices. Roll each slice of bacon around a strip of steak. Secure with a toothpick. Brown bacon-wrapped steak in 2 tablespoons of oil. Mix all sauce ingredients together in a blender. Add sauce to meat and simmer 45 minutes. Serve with vegetables.

Delicious with fresh flour tortillas.

Jeannie Burns   *Los Osos Junior High School, Los Osos*

Shredded Beef Burritos

Serves at least 10

5 lbs. chuck roast
3 tablespoons fat from roast drippings
2 large onions, chopped
1 can (4 oz.) green chiles, chopped
2 cans (7 oz. each) chile salsa
¼ teaspoon garlic powder
4 tablespoons flour
2 teaspoons salt

1 teaspoon ground cumin
skimmed meat juices
flour tortillas
lettuce
tomatoes
black olives
guacamole
sour cream

Roast beef in 200°F oven, covered, with no seasonings for 12 hours. Shred beef. Put drippings in the refrigerator. When fat hardens, keep 3 tablespoons of it. Keep drippings. In a large fry pan, put 3 tablespoons fat, and chopped onions, saute until clear. Add green chiles, chile salsa, garlic powder, flour, salt, and ground cumin. Cook for 1 minute. Add meat and meat drippings. Heat throughout. You can refrigerate or freeze at this point, or continue on for burritos.

Put ¼ cup meat mixture in middle of tortilla. Fold up to make a rectangle. Place on a bed of shredded lettuce, garnish with tomatoes, olives, guacamole, and sour cream.

Or . . . put meat mixture in pita bread with sprouts.

Or . . . add shredded or diced cooked potatoes to meat mixture; enclose in a pastry round and bake in oven (350°F) for 20 minutes.

Kelly Goughnour   **Yreka High School, Yreka**

Quick and Easy Burritos Ⓜ

Serves 6 to 8

1 lb. ground beef
½ cup onion, chopped
¼ teaspoon garlic powder
salt and pepper to taste

1 can (16 oz.) refried beans
1 dozen flour tortillas
½ lb. Monterey jack cheese, shredded

In a large skillet, brown ground beef and drain off fat. Add chopped onion, garlic powder, salt and pepper, simmer for 5 minutes. Add refried beans and bring these ingredients to a gentle boil. Turn off heat. Warm flour tortillas individually on low burner; lay on breadboard and put a large spoonful of beef mixture in center. Add small handful of shredded cheese and wrap tortilla around each mixture. Place in a 9 x 13 inch serving dish. May need 10 to 15 minutes of "warm-up" in a low oven before serving, about 300°F. Each burrito may be wrapped in waxed paper and frozen also. Can be warmed in the microwave oven at HIGH power for 1 to 2 minutes before serving.

Jean L. Dempsey   **Santa Paula High School, Santa Paula**

Big Burrito Party

Serves 8 to 12 (4 feet long)

1 12 inch wide board of desired length (6 to 8 feet)
1 package extra large flour tortillas (12 inch size), heated
extra strong aluminum foil
1 large can refried beans, heated
2 to 2½ lbs. ground beef, browned with spices added (onions optional),
* hot (recipe below)*
1½ lbs. cheddar cheese, grated
6 to 8 green onions, finely chopped
4 medium tomatoes, chopped
6 to 9 oz. chile salsa (your degree of hotness)
1 large (32 oz.) size sour cream, stirred
guacamole, made from 4 or 5 avocados (recipe below)
½ to 1 can pitted black olives, chopped

NOTE: Double or triple recipe for more people

Assembly Directions: Cover the board with the foil and place on table top (or between two card tables if very long burrito). Wrap the tortillas in a slightly damp clean kitchen towel and then aluminum foil. Heat in a 300°F oven for 20 minutes or until warm. Chop or prepare all food products and place in bowls when ready to assemble. Recipes will follow . . .

Each guest should have something to do to assemble the burrito. Be sure to give explicit directions to each person. Everything should be ready before you begin!

1. Place the tortillas on the foil overlapping about one-third.
2. Quickly spread a 3 inch wide strip of hot refried beans, then top with:
3. Hot meat mixture, then add
4. Half of the grated cheese.
5. Top with green onions,
6. Add the chopped tomatoes,
7. Sprinkle on the salsa,
8. Add the rest of the cheese.
9. Top with half the sour cream.
10. Roll up the tortillas (first one side then the other). Pat down gently to hold all together. Everyone should help with this step.
11. Quickly top with the guacamole,
12. Then spread a 1 inch strip of sour cream down the middle and
13. Finally sprinkle the chopped olives over the sour cream and guacamole.

Cut into 2 to 4 inch wide servings.

Guacamole:

4 to 5 avocados, peeled and
* mashed*
2 tomatoes, chopped finely
¼ medium onion, finely chopped

6 drops tabasco
1 small clove garlic, finely chopped
½ cup sour cream

Mix all ingredients together. Cover with 1 tablespoon of lemon juice, if not used immediately.

(continued next page)

Ground Beef Mixture

2 to 2½ lbs. ground beef, browned
   and drained
1 can (8 oz.) of tomato sauce

1 teaspoon cumin
1 tablespoons salsa

Mix all ingredients together and simmer.

Rhonda Rohde   *Warren High School, Downey*

Mexican Stir Fry

Serves 4

1 lb. beef flank steak
2 tablespoons oil
1 teaspoon ground cumin
1 teaspoon garlic
1 teaspoon oregano

1 sweet red pepper, cut into
   thin strips
1 medium onion, chopped
1 to 2 jalapeno chiles, seeded
   and cut into slivers

Toppings:
shredded cheese
chopped tomato
guacamole

salsa
1 package taco shells or tortillas

Cut beef diagonally across grain into ⅛ inch slices. Combine oil, cumin, garlic, and oregano. Heat 1 tablespoon oil mixture in wok. Add red pepper, onion, and jalapeno chiles. Stir fry over medium heat for 2 to 3 minutes. Remove from pan and reserve. Stir fry beef strips, half at a time, in remaining oil mixture 1 to 2 minutes. Return vegetables to wok and heat through.

Use for tacos or tostadas. Top with desired toppings.

Rebecca Oppen Tice   *Dana Hills High School, Dana Point*

Tijuana Pie

Serves 8

1½ lb. ground beef
1 onion, chopped
1 garlic clove, chopped
1 teaspoon salt
¼ teaspoon pepper
vegetable oil
6 corn tortillas
1 can (10 oz.) enchilada sauce

1 can (8 oz.) tomato sauce
¾ lb. (3 cups) cheddar cheese,
   grated
2 cans (16 oz. each) chile
   seasoned beans
1 can (16 oz.) corn, drained,
   or 1¾ cup fresh corn
1 can (6 oz.) olives, drained

Brown meat, onion and garlic in skillet. Drain. Season with salt and pepper. Wipe the inside of crockpot with oil. Place one tortilla on the bottom of the crockpot. Make alternate layers of meat, sauces and cheese. Top with another tortilla, then beans, cheese, corn and a few olives. Continue layers, ending with cheese and olives. cover. Cook on low for 5 to 7 hours. Serve with additional tortillas.

Variations: Add green chiles, and substitute green olives for black olives; chicken, turkey or chorizo for beef. Tasty, hearty and easy!

Gennan Taylor   *Bonita High School, La Verne*

Mexican Pile-On

Serves 8

1 lb. ground beef
1 small onion, chopped
2 cloves garlic, mashed
1 teaspoon salt
1 teaspoon MSG (Accent)
1 teaspoon oregano
1 teaspoon ground cumin

1 teaspoon chili powder
1 can (6 oz.) tomato paste
2 cans water
1 can (8 oz.) tomato sauce
2 tablespoons sugar, to taste
1 cup rice, cooked

Brown ground beef. Add onion and garlic; cook until soft. Add remaining ingredients, except rice; simmer 10 minutes or until flavors blend. Add rice. (This much can be done ahead and reheated). To serve, put each of the following in a separate bowl on a buffet. Guests serve themselves, piling items on their plate:

Fritos
meat mixture
cheese (combination of cheddar
   and monterey jack, grated)
chopped head lettuce
green onion, sliced thin

tomatoes, quartered or eighths
avocado slices
chile salsa (purchased)
sour cream (special recipe below)
sliced olives

Sour Cream Topping (Serves 8 or more)

1 pint sour cream
1/4 cup onion, chopped
1/2 teaspoon garlic, mashed in
   1 teaspoon salt
Mix all ingredients together

1/4 cup cilantro (Mexican or
   Chinese parsley), finely chopped
pinch of sugar

Fun fare for a party. For pot luck, have each guest bring a part of the meal.

Joan Irvine   **Upland High School, Upland**

Supper Nachos (You Create Your Own)

ground beef, cooked,
   crumbled and drained
refried beans, heated
Tortilla chips
onion, chopped
green chiles, chopped
jack cheese, grated

cheddar cheese, grated
ripe olives, sliced
tomatoes, chopped
salsa
guacamole
sour cream

Prepare ingredients listed above. Put in separate bowls. Place ground beef and beans on a heating tray to keep warm. Family or guests serve themselves buffet style so they create their own supper nachos. Put tortilla chips on plate first and build their own nachos as desired. Serve with a green salad and you have a complete meal.

Terrific for a large party and the hostess can relax because it can all be done in advance!

Susan Lefler   **Ramona Junior High School, Chino**

Super Supper Nachos   Ⓜ

Serves 6

1 lb. lean ground beef
1 package (1¼ oz.) taco seasoning
   mix
⅓ cup water
1 can (16 oz.) refried beans

1 package (8 oz.) cheddar cheese,
   shredded
1 carton (8 oz.) sour cream
¼ cup black olives, sliced
2 green onions, sliced
round tortilla chips

Place ground beef in batter bowl. Cover with a paper towel. Microwave on HIGH for 3 minutes. Stir with a wooden spoon, Microwave 2 to 4 minutes more until meat is no longer pink. Remove from oven. Drain grease.

Stir in taco seasoning mix and water. Set aside. Spread the beans in the bottom of a 6 x 10 inch glass baking dish or on 2 paper plates. Evenly spread the meat mixture over the refried beans. Sprinkle with shredded cheese. Microwave on HIGH for 3 to 5 minutes, until the cheese is melted. Carefully remove from the oven.

Spread sour cream down the middle only. Sprinkle olive slices and onion slices over the sour cream. Decorate with tortilla chips; stand them around the edge of the casserole. Serve additional tortilla chips in a basket on the side.

Shirley Marshman   **West Middle School, Downey**

Carol's Burritos

Serves 6

3 tablespoons cooking oil
¾ lb. stew beef, cut in ½ inch
   pieces
¾ lb pork shoulder, cut in ½ inch
   pieces
1 cup onion, chopped
1 cup garlic, crushed

1 teaspoon salt
1½ cups water
1 can (4 oz.) green chiles, drained
1 can refried beans
¼ cup cheddar cheese, shredded
12 flour tortillas

Heat 2 tablespoons oil in a large skillet; cook beef, pork, and onion until meat is browned and onion is tender. Add garlic, salt and water; heat to boiling. Reduce heat and simmer, covered, for 2 hours or until meat is tender and begins to fall apart. Add chiles and, with fork, gently flake meat. Continue cooking, uncovered, until all liquid has evaporated. Heat refried beans in 1 tablespoon oil. Add cheese; heat until cheese is melted.

In the center of each tortilla, spread about 2 tablespoons bean mixture in a thin layer. Spoon about 2 tablespoons meat mixture near one edge of tortilla. Roll up, folding ends securely, forming a rectangular roll. Place burritos on a cookie sheet; cover with foil. Heat in preheated 325°F oven for 15 minutes. Serve with taco sauce or chili hot dog sauce. Eat like a sandwich.

Good to make ahead and freeze for future use.

Karen Lopez   **San Luis Obispo High School, San Luis Obispo**

Supper Nachos

½ lb. ground beef
½ onion, chopped
½ teaspoon seasoned salt
¼ teaspoon cumin
1 can (16 oz.) refried beans
½ package Lawry's Taco
  Seasoning Mix

1 cup jack cheese, grated
½ can (4 oz.) green chiles,
  chopped
½ cup cheddar cheese, grated
6 tablespoons Lawry's Chunky
  Taco Sauce
Tortilla chips

Garnish with any or all of the following:

½ cup guacamole
½ cup sour cream

¼ cup green onions, chopped
½ cup ripe olives, sliced

Brown meat and onion; drain well and add seasoned salt and cumin. Combine beans, taco seasoning mix and jack cheese; mix well. Spread beans in a 7 x 11 inch baking pan. Cover with meat mixture. Sprinkle chiles over meat; top with cheddar cheese. Pour chunky taco sauce over cheese. Bake, uncovered at 400°F for 20 minutes or until thoroughly heated. Tuck tortilla chips around edge of platter and garnish as desired.

Phyllis Chutuk   **Oceanside High School, Oceanside**

Mexican Pizza

Serves 8

1 lb. ground beef
1 can (16 oz.) tomatoes
1 can (6 oz.) tomato paste
½ cup onion, chopped
¼ cup water
2 tablespoons chili powder

1¼ teaspoon salt
¼ teaspoon pepper
12 corn tortillas
2 cups cheddar cheese, shredded
1 cup lettuce, shredded
1 avocado, sliced

Brown meat, drain and stir in tomatoes, tomato paste, onion, water and seasonings. Simmer 10 minutes. Cover bottom and sides of a 14 inch pizza pan with tortillas. Spread meat sauce evenly over tortillas. Bake for 20 minutes at 350°F. Now sprinkle with 1 cup cheese and continue baking until cheese is melted. To serve, top with combined lettuce and remaining cheese. Garnish with avocado.

Marie Humphrey   **Grant School, Escondido**

Mexicali Burger

Serves 1

4 oz. ground beef patty
1 hamburger bun
green leaf lettuce
red onion, thinly sliced

tomato slice
guacamole
La Victoria Marinated Jalapeno
  Peppers, optional
desired La Victoria Salsa

Broil beef patty to desired doneness; toast bun if desired. Place burger on bun half; top with remaining ingredients as desired.

La Victoria Foods, Inc.   **City of Industry**

100 M.P.H. Chili

Serves 6

1 lb. lean pork (1/2 inch cubes)
1 lb. stew beef (1 inch cubes)
1/2 cup flour
2 tablespoons shortening
1 onion, sliced
3 cups beef stock (6 cubes)
8 oz. can tomatillas
5 1/2 oz. green chiles, chopped
1 1/2 oz. tomato paste

1/4 teaspoon garlic powder
2 1/2 teaspoons cumin
1/2 teaspoon salt
1 1/4 teaspoon black pepper
1 1/4 teaspoon chili powder
1 1/4 teaspoon cayenne pepper
3 teaspoons paprika
1 1/2 teaspoon Masa Harina or
   cornstarch
8 oz. pureed tomatoes

Dust meat in flour. Brown in shortening. Saute onions. Place meat and onions in a heavy pot. Add all ingredients, except Masa Harina and tomatoes (pureed). Stir well, bring to a boil; reduce heat and simmer, stirring occasionally until the meat is tender (approximately 45 minutes). Add pureed tomatoes, bring back to a boil, add 1 1/2 teaspoon Masa Harina, stir well and simmer for 15 minutes.

This recipe was Baxter's Restaurant competition with other restaurants in 1981 in Orange County. It won first prize.

Connie Salvo   **San Gabriel High School, San Gabriel**

Crepes Ensenada

Serves 6

12 flour tortillas
12 slices (thin) ham

3 ortega chiles, seeded and
   cut in fourths
1 lb. jack cheese, cut in pieces

Sauce:
1/2 cup butter or margarine
1/2 cup flour
1 quart milk
3 to 4 cups cheddar cheese, grated

1/2 teaspoon mustard
   (dry or prepared)
1/2 teaspoon salt
1/4 teaspoon pepper

Roll tortilla with ham slice (I use Danola deli ham, but thinly sliced leftovers will do.), chile strip (1/4 of large chile) and a piece of jack cheese, cut to the size of your little finger. Place tortilla rolls in a greased baking dish, seam side down. Can be covered and refrigerated at this point up to 24 hours in advance.

Sauce: Melt butter or margarine. Add flour, remove from heat, whisk in milk and replace on burner and cook over medium heat, stirring constantly, until mixture thickens and reaches boiling point. Add grated cheddar and mustard, salt and pepper. Pour over rolled tortillas and bake for 40 minutes at 350°F and serve. GREAT!

This is great with a green salad and fresh fruit for dessert. I can prepare the sauce and the tortillas ahead of time and combine them just before baking. "Yummy", is the comment I usually get!

Ellen Black-Eacker   **Nogales High School, La Puente**

Mexican Monte Carlo Sandwich

Serves 6

2 cans (7 oz.) green chile salsa
1 1/4 lbs. of ground beef
12 1/2 inch thick slices sour dough
　bread
1 can (7 oz.) whole green chiles,
　split

4 oz. Monterey jack cheese, grated
2 eggs, beaten
1 cup milk
butter or margarine

Combine 1 can salsa with ground beef. Shape into 6 patties. Broil until cooked as desired. Place cooked patty on bread slice. Top with part of whole chile, 1 tablespoon grated cheese and another slice of bread. Combine eggs and milk. Dip both sides of sandwich in mixture. Melt butter in skillet. Cook sandwich on both sides until golden brown and cheese is melted. Heat remaining salsa. Serve with sandwich.

Betty Jo Smith　　　　　　　　*Tahoe-Truckee High School, Truckee*

Quick Chorizo Quiche

Serves 4

Butter or margarine
1/4 cup tomato sauce
1 teaspoon chili sauce (or salsa)
1 12 inch tortilla
oil
1/2 lb. chorizo

4 eggs
1 cup cream
1 tablespoon cilantro, minced
1 1/2 cups monterey jack cheese,
　grated
1 tomato, chopped

Generously butter a 9 inch pie pan. Mix tomato sauce with salsa. Fry tortilla in hot oil until **slightly** crisp, drain on paper towel, place in pie pan, cupping up edges to fit. Spread tortilla with tomato sauce mixture. Fry chorizo, casing removed, until broken into small pieces and browned. Drain well. Sprinkle over tortilla. Beat eggs and cream. Stir in cilantro, cheese and tomato. Pour into tortilla. Bake at 375°F for 30 minutes or until eggs test done with blade or knife.

Diedre Simon　　　　　　　　*Norwalk High School, Norwalk*

Chile Verde

Serves 4

2 lbs. pork stew meat, cut into
　1 inch cubes
2 tablespoons cooking oil
1 cup green bell pepper,
　finely chopped
4 green onions, sliced

3 cloves garlic, minced
2 jars (12 oz.) jars La Victoria
　Green Chili Salsa
1 can (13 oz.) La Victoria
　Tomatilla Entero
hot cooked rice

Garnishes: La Victoria Green Chili Salsa, sliced green onion, cilantro sprigs

Place meat in Dutch oven with water to cover. Bring to boiling; reduce heat. Simmer, covered, 1 hour. Cool; drain. In same pan heat oil. Brown meat on all sides. Add bell pepper, onion, and garlic; cook till tender. Stir in Salsa and Tomatillos; cover and simmer 30 minutes. Serve over hot rice. Garnish if desired.

La Victoria Foods, Inc.　　　　　　　　*City of Industry*

Chuck's Chile Verde

Serves 6 to 8

3 lbs. pork shoulder, cubed
3 tablespoons olive oil
½ cup bell pepper, chopped
¼ teaspoon garlic powder
1 can (1 lb.) stewed tomatoes
1 can (8 oz.) tomato sauce
½ cup water
1 can (4 oz.) Ortega chiles, diced

2 tablespoons dried parsley
¼ teaspoon sugar
⅛ teaspoon ground cloves
1 teaspoon ground cumin
¾ cup beef broth
¼ cup lemon juice
salt

Brown pork in heated oil; remove with a slotted spoon and reserve. In pan drippings, saute bell pepper and garlic until soft. Add a little more oil if needed. In a large, 5 quart pan, combine tomatoes and their liquid, tomato sauce, water, green chiles, parsley, seasonings, beef broth and lemon juice. Bring to a boil, then reduce heat to simmer. Add browned meat and bell pepper. Cover and simmer for 2 hours, stirring occasionally.

Remove cover; simmer for about 45 minutes more until sauce is reduced to thickness you wish and meat is very tender. Taste and add salt.

My husband created this recipe and serves it over cheese enchiladas. Everyone always asks for his recipe.

Carole Delap   **Golden West High School, Visalia**

Lawry's Chile Verde

Serves 6

1½ lbs. lean pork, cut into ½ x 3 inch strips
1 tablespoon shortening
1 can (16 oz.) whole tomatoes, broken up
3 cans (4 oz. each) whole green chiles, de-veined and seeded,
    cut into narrow lengthwise strips.
¼ teaspoon oregano
½ teaspoon Lawry's Garlic Powder with Parsley
1 tablespoon Lawry's Minced Onion with Green Onion Flakes
1 package Lawry's Brown Gravy Mix
¼ cup water
Lawry's Seasoned Salt, to taste

Brown pork strips in shortening. Add remaining ingredients and bring to a boil. Simmer covered 1 to 1½ hours, stirring occasionally. Remove cover and simmer 10 to 15 minutes until slightly thickened. Serve over rice or use as a filling for burritos.

I picked this recipe up several years ago on a tour of Lawry's California Center.

Pam Ford   **Temecula Valley High School, Rancho California**

Chile Quiche

Serves 4

2 (thin) chorizo sausages or
   1 (fat) one
3 eggs
1¾ cup hot milk
1 teaspoon salt
2 cups Monterey jack cheese,
   grated

½ cup green chiles, finely chopped
butter or oil
3 green onions, chopped
⅓ cup black olives, chopped
5 tortillas, cooked

Remove sausage meat from casing and crumble meat. Fry until browned, breaking up with a fork. Drain well. Beat eggs and stir in milk, sausage, cheese, and chiles. Butter or oil pie pan. Overlap the 5 tortillas in the bottom of the pan. Spread mixture on top of tortilla pie shell. Sprinkle onions and olives on top of mixture. Bake on lowest shelf of preheated 350°F to 375°F oven and bake for 35 minutes or until mixture is set in the center and nicely brown. Let stand 10 minutes before cutting. Serve warm.

Nan Paul   **Grant Middle School, Escondido**

Breakfast Tacos

Serves as many as you like

To serve one:

1 tablespoon butter
corn tortillas
egg
salt (½ teaspoon)
pepper (a dash)
sausage
bacon or ham

jack cheese
cheddar cheese
avocado
green chile, chopped
green onion, chopped
tomatoes, chopped
sour cream

Melt 1 tablespoon of butter in an omelet pan. Use medium heat. Dip a corn tortilla in egg batter made from: 1 egg slightly beaten, ½ teaspoon salt and a dash of pepper. Use a small bowl. Fry one side of the tortilla until golden brown (about ½ minute). Flip the tortilla over and add the ingredients you like to your tortilla:

    a. *Sausage, bacon, ham — cooked, crumbled into pieces*
    b. *Cheese (jack or cheddar), grated*
    c. *Avocado, chopped*
    d. *Green chile, chopped*
    e. *Green onion, chopped*
    f. *Tomatoes, chopped*

Top with a teaspoon of sour cream. Fold over the unused side of the tortilla and cook until the cheese is melted. Top with one more spoonful of sour cream.

Mary Ann Baldiviez   **El Camino Junior High School, Santa Maria**

Tostadas Sonorenses
(Tostadas, Sonora Style)

Serves 6

6 corn tortillas
1 cup fat
4 Mexican sausages
  (can use chorizo)
1 small head lettuce, shredded
1 large onion, chop half, slice half

3 ounce package cream cheese
1 tablespoon olive oil
1 teaspoon vinegar
1 teaspoon salt
tomato cheese sauce
  (recipe follows)

Fry tortillas one by one in fat until they are golden in color. Remove and drain on paper toweling. Fry the sausages in the same shortening. Drain and chop very fine.

On each hot tortilla, place a bit of shredded lettuce, a tablespoon of the chopped sausage, a teaspoon of chopped onion and a tablespoon of cream cheese. Season with oil, vinegar and salt. Cover with tomato cheese sauce and garnish with sliced onion.

Tomato and Cheese Sauce

2 large tomatoes
1 small green chile
2 tablespoons fat
3 ounce cream cheese, sliced

Heat tomatoes in water to cover. Drain tomatoes, save ½ cup water. Peel tomatoes and grind with chile. Add fat, cream cheese and the reserved ½ cup water. Cook about 4 minutes.

This recipe is from Juan J. Denis, a native of Sonora, Mexico, also an instructor at CSUS.

Gloria Walker   **Casa Roble Fundamental High School, Orangevale**

Meat Loaf Helena

Serves 6

2 lbs. ground beef
1 can (2.3 oz.) sliced ripe olives,
  drained
2 carrots, peeled and shredded
1 green onion, thinly sliced
1 teaspoon salt
1 egg, beaten

2 to 4 tablespoons La Victoria
  Whole Marinated Jalapeno
  Peppers*, finely chopped
2 slices cheddar or American
  cheese
4 La Victoria Whole Marinated
  Jalapeno Peppers

Stir together all ingredients except cheese and whole peppers. Mix lightly but thoroughly. Shape mixture into a loaf, or pack lightly but firmly into a 9 x 5 inch loaf pan. Bake in a 375°F oven for 1 hour. Arrange cheese slices on top; garnish with whole peppers. Slice to serve.

*Rinse chiles and remove seeds before mincing. Wash hands thoroughly after handling chiles; keep hands away from eyes.

La Victoria Foods, Inc.   **City of Industry**

Chile Colorado Burritos

Yields 1 dozen

12 dried California Chiles
3 cups beef stock, fat removed
3 lbs. beef chuck, cubed
6 tablespoons flour
fat
salt to tast
4 cloves garlic

2 tablespoons oregano
1/2 teaspoon cumin
1 package large flour tortillas
cheese, grated
1 onion, chopped
1 large can refried beans
1 large can LaPalma enchilada
   sauce

Soak chiles in hot water for 35 to 40 minutes. Remove stems and seeds, discard. Grind chiles and some of the beef stock in blender to make a paste. Put through a sieve to eliminate bits of peel. Dredge meat cubes in flour. Brown in fat, seasoned to taste with salt; add garlic, oregano, cumin, chile paste and remaining beef stock. Cover and simmer for 2 to 3 hours. Heat large flour tortillas on griddle until soft. Place some of the filling just below center. Place cheese, chopped onion, then top with refried beans. Fold the sides of the tortilla to center then fold bottom flap over filling and roll.

Preheat oven to 375°F. Place on lightly greased cookie sheet. Cover each with a bit of sauce, sprinkle with cheese and heat until cheese melts. Before serving, place a bit of sour cream or guacamole on top.

Barbara Boling   *Orange High School, Orange*

Poultry & Fish

"Coach Yancey's Favorite Dish"

Serves 6

1 lb. turkey burger
1 small onion
1 can (8 oz.) Mexican style
  tomatoes
1 small can green chiles, diced

1 can Mexican corn
1 package (6 oz.) cheddar cheese
1 package corn tortillas
1 bag tortilla style chips

Brown turkey burger and onion in skillet; drain. Add can of tomatoes, diced green chiles and corn to turkey burger. Set aside. Grate cheese, set aside. Layer tortillas on bottom of a round casserole dish. Pour in ⅓ of the meat and tomato mixture. Sprinkle cheese on top, then tortillas again. Repeat layers. Top with cheese and crushed tortilla chips.

1987 water polo "Coach of the Year" - Steve Yancy, loves the stuff. He can eat the entire casserole in one sitting. Top with guacamole and sour cream.

Lisa Yancey   *San Clemente High School, San Clemente*

Chicken or Beef Enchiladas

Serves 4

1 small onion
2 large cans (7 oz. each) green
  chiles, diced
½ teaspoon cumin
oil
2 tablespoon flour

2 cups sour cream
3 cups (¾ lb.) jack cheese,
  shredded
12 corn tortillas
shredded cooked beef or
  shredded cooked chicken

Combine onion, chiles, and cumin in a small amount of oil and cook over medium heat for about 15 minutes. Mix in flour and blend in 1 cup sour cream, stir until simmered. Remove from heat and add one cup cheese. Make each enchilada by stirring beef or chicken into sauce. Fill and roll each tortilla. Bake in long casserole, uncovered, at 375°F until hot in center, about 15 minutes (25 minutes if chilled). Sprinkle remaining cheese on top and return to oven for 5 minutes or until cheese melts.

Sybil Schweighauser   *Thomas Jefferson Junior High School, Wasco*

Chicken-Sour Cream Enchilada

Serves 6

⅔ cup sour cream
⅔ can cream of chicken soup
1⅓ cup chicken, cooked and diced
1⅓ oz. green chiles, diced

⅛ teaspoon cumin
salt to taste
6 flour tortillas
oil
⅔ cup mild cheddar cheese, grated

In a small bowl, mix ⅓ cup sour cream and ⅓ cup soup. Set aside. Combine remaining sour cream, soup, chicken, chiles, cumin and salt to taste. Blend well. Soften tortillas in hot oil. Spoon chicken mixture into tortillas and roll to close. Place fold side down on greased baking dish. Top with reserved soup and sour cream. Top with grated cheese.

Sue Nall   *Temple City High School, Temple City*

Chicken Enchiladas in Cheese Cream

Serves 6

2 whole (about 1 lb.) boneless,
  skinned chicken breasts, halved
1/2 cup water
2 cloves garlic, thinly sliced
1 large onion, finely chopped
3 tablespoons butter or margarine
1 clove garlic, finely chopped
2 cans (3 1/2 oz. each) whole green
  chiles, seeded, rinsed, chopped
1 tablespoon chili powder
1/2 teaspoon ground cumin

1/2 teaspoon salt
1/4 teaspoon leaf oregano, crushed
1/4 teaspoon pepper
1/4 cup all-purpose flour
1 cup chicken broth, canned
1 cup heavy cream
1/2 lb. monterey jack cheese,
  shredded
1/4 to 1/3 cup vegetable oil
12 corn tortillas, 6 inch
6 green onions, trimmed and sliced

Place chicken breasts in medium sized saucepan. Add water and sliced garlic. Cover and bring to a simmer. Cook just until tender. Cool. Remove chicken and reserve broth. Cut chicken into thin julienne strips. Set aside in a bowl.

Saute onion in butter or margarine in medium size skillet just until soft, about 5 minutes. Add chopped garlic, saute 1 minute. Add chiles, chili powder, cumin, salt, oregano, and pepper. Cook 1 minute. Stir in flour until well combined; cook 1 minute, stirring.

Stir in the reserved chicken broth from the cooked chicken, 1 cup chicken broth canned and heavy cream. Cook over medium heat, stirring frequently until mixture thickens, about 10 minutes. Remove from heat. Stir in 1 cup of shredded cheese until melted. Combine 1 cup cheese sauce with reserved chicken. Preheat oven to 400°F.

Heat vegetable oil in a small skillet until hot. Dip tortillas, one at a time, in hot oil just until limp, about 5 to 10 seconds on each side. Don't let them become crisp. Place on a work surface. Divide chicken filling equally along the center of each tortilla and top each with sliced green onion. Roll up tortillas and place seam side down, in 2 rows in a 13 x 9 x 2 inch baking pan. Pour remaining cheese sauce evenly over tortillas and sprinkle with remaining 1 cup of cheese.

Bake at 400°F for 20 minutes or until bubbly.

It looks like a lot of work and a lot of ingredients, but it really isn't. And . . . it tastes so good!

Barbara Behrends   **Mojave High School, Mojave**

Turkey Enchiladas with Sour Cream

Serves 6

2 cans (4 oz. each) green chiles,
diced
1 large clove garlic, minced
2 tablespoons olive oil
1½ lbs. fresh, ripe tomtoes
2 cups onions, chopped
2 teaspoons salt

½ teaspoon oregano
½ cup water
3 cups cooked turkey, shredded
2 cups sour cream
2 cups cheddar cheese, shredded
⅓ cup salad oil
12 corn tortillas

Saute chiles with garlic in heated olive oil. Peel and chop tomatoes and add with onions, 1 teaspoon of salt, oregano and water. Simmer, uncovered for 30 minutes. Set aside. Combine turkey with sour cream, cheese and remaining one teaspoon salt. Heat oil and dip tortillas, one at a time, in hot oil just until limp. Fill tortillas with turkey mixture, roll up, and arrange seam side down in a shallow baking pan. Pour chile sauce over the top and bake in a 350°F oven for about 20 minutes, or until heated through.

Great use of leftover turkey. Could use chicken as well.

Julie Shelburne   **Tulare Union High School, Tulare**

White Enchiladas

Serves 4 to 6

*1 dozen corn tortillas
oil to soften tortillas
2 cups cooked chicken
1 small can green chiles*

*1 can cream of chicken soup
1 cup sour cream
½ lb. (2 cups) jack cheese,
shredded*

Dip tortillas in hot oil to soften. Put 2 tablespoons of chicken on tortillas. Combine green chiles and cream of chicken soup; reserve ⅓ mixture to pour over top. Combine sour cream, jack cheese, ⅔ soup and chile mixture. Spread desired amount over chicken/tortilla. Roll into enchilada shape and place seam side down on pan. Continue until all tortillas are used. Cover enchiladas with ⅓ reserved soup and chile mixture. Cover with grated jack cheese. Bake for 30 minutes at 350°F, in a 9 x 13 inch baking dish.

My students love this!

Marty Thweatt   **Monte Vista High School, Spring Valley**

Mexican Roll-ups

Serves 2

*2 (4 oz.) chicken breasts, boned
and skinned
2 oz. Monterey jack cheese,
cut into 2 long strips*

*2 whole green chiles
3 tablespoons bread crumbs
1 teaspooon chili powder
4 teaspoons low calorie margarine*

Dip chicken in water. Wrap cheese and green chile in chicken breast. Make into a roll. Coat each roll with bread crumbs and chili powder. Refrigerate 1 hour. Place 2 teaspoons low calorie margarine on top of each chicken roll. Bake in 400°F oven for 20 to 25 minutes.

Favorite weight-watcher recipe.

Darlene V. Brown   Golden Valley Intermediate School, San Bernardino

White Enchiladas with Guacamole

Serves 6

2 3 lb. broiler fryers
3 cans (7 oz. each) green chiles
  diced
2½ lb. jack cheese, grated

12 flour tortillas
½ cup oil
1½ pints whipping cream

Cook chicken; bone and cube. Combine chicken with chiles and ¾ of the cheese. Soften tortillas in oil. Heat cream. Dip each tortilla in cream. Put ½ cup of chicken and cheese mixture in center of each tortilla. Fold sides over and place seam side down in a greased baking dish. Pour remaining cream over and sprinkle with rest of cheese. Bake at 450°F for 30 to 45 minutes, or until golden brown.

Guacamole (to be served with White Enchiladas)

2 large ripe avocados
1 tablespoon lemon juice
salt to taste

2 tablespoons onion, grated
1 teaspoon chili powder
½ cup mayonnaise

Mash avocados and add rest of ingredients, except mayonnaise. Mix well. Cover mixture with mayonnaise, sealing edges. Chill for 20 minutes. Blend in mayonnaise and serve.

Eleanor Magorien   *El Toro High School, El Toro*

Turkey Olive Enchiladas

Serves 6

3 tablespoons butter
2 cups mushrooms, sliced
½ cup onion, chopped
2 to 3 cups turkey or chicken,
  cooked and diced
1 can (10½ oz.) cream of chicken
  soup, undiluted
1 cup dairy sour cream

½ cup pimento stuffed olives,
  sliced
½ cup slivered almonds, toasted
1½ to 2 teaspoons chili powder
12 corn tortillas
oil
½ cup cheddar cheese, grated

Melt butter in a large saucepan. Add mushrooms and onion; saute over medium heat, stirring occasionally, until onion is tender. Remove from heat and stir in turkey, undiluted soup, sour cream, olives, almonds, and chili powder. Briefly cook tortillas in hot oil until softened; then drain on paper towels. For each enchilada, place about ⅓ cup turkey mixture in center of each tortilla. Bring opposite sides of each tortilla up over turkey mixture, overlapping edges at center. Arrange seamside down in an ungreased 9 x 13 inch baking dish. Spoon remaining turkey mixture down center of each enchilada. Sprinkle cheese on top. Bake at 400°F for about 25 minutes or until hot.

Clyle Alt   *Bell Gardens High School, Bell Gardens*

mmmm. . . Chicken Enchiladas

Serves 6

12 corn tortillas
2 cans (10 oz.) green enchilada
  sauce, heated
2 cups chicken or turkey, diced
1/2 pint sour cream

1/2 cup green onions, (including
  green tops), chopped
1/2 of 4 oz. size can green chiles,
  chopped
1/2 teaspoon seasoned salt
3/4 cup cheddar cheese, shredded

Soft-fry tortillas according to directions to soften. Dip tortillas, one at a time, with tongs, into heated green enchilada sauce. Place tortillas in large shallow baking dish. Meanwhile, in large mixing bowl, combine chicken, sour cream, green onions, chiles and salt, mixing well. Spoon 1/4 cup chicken mixture into center of each tortilla

Roll each tortilla around filling and place flap side diwon in same shallow baking dish. Spoon remaining enchilada sauce over rolled tortillas. Sprinkle with cheese. Bake, uncovered, in 350°F oven for 15 minutes to heat through and melt cheese.

Marcia Nye   *Woodrow Wilson High School, Long Beach*

Mexican Chicken Rollups (Crescent Style)

Serves 8

1 1/2 teaspoons cornmeal
2 1/4 cups cooked chicken or turkey, cubed
1 cup sharp cheddar cheese, grated
1/2 cup sour cream
1/2 cup ripe olives, sliced
1/2 cup green onion, chopped
1 can (4 oz.) green chiles, chopped
2 cans (8 oz. each) Pillsbury Refrigerated Quick Crescent Dinner Rolls
1 egg white
1 tablespoon water
1 teaspoon cornmeal
1 jar (12 oz.) red or green chile salsa

Heat oven to 375°F. Lightly grease cookie sheet; sprinkle with 1 1/2 teaspoons cornmeal. In a large bowl, combine chicken, cheese, sour cream, olives, onions, and chiles; mix well. Separate dough into 8 rectangles. Firmly press perforations to seal. Spoon about 1/2 cup chicken mixture on each rectangle; spread to within 1 inch of edge. Starting at longest side, roll up jelly roll fashion; pinch edge to seal. Place seam side down on prepared cookie sheet.

In a small bowl, beat egg white and water; brush over each rollup. Sprinkle with 1 teaspoon cornmeal. Bake at 375°F for 20 to 25 minutes or until golden brown. Top with chile salsa. If desired, serve with sour cream or guacamole.

Sue Zallar   *Capistrano Valley High School, Mission Viejo*

Taco Chicken

Serves 6

1 can condensed cream of chicken
  soup
⅓ cup chile sauce
⅓ cup water
3 drops of tabasco sauce

3 whole chicken breasts,
  split in half (about 3 lbs.)
⅓ cup flour
3 cups taco flavored corn chips, or
  tortilla chips, finely crushed
2 tablespoons butter, melted

Mix soup, chile sauce, water and tabasco sauce. Dust chicken with flour and dip in soup mixture. Roll chicken in crushed corn or tortilla chips. Place on rack in shallow baking pan. Drizzle chicken with melted butter. Bake at 400°F for one hour or until done.

Joanne Fial   *East Middle School, Downey*

Tacos Verde, Blanco y Colorado

Serves 6 to 12

1 small onion, chopped
1 tablespoon oil
1 can tomato sauce or puree
1 tablespoon (or more) chile relish
salt to taste
12 tortillas
oil for frying

2 cups cooked, cubed chicken
  (white meat)
¼ cup parmesan cheese, grated
1 cup guacamole
½ pint sour cream
pickled pearl onions or onion rings

For sauce, wilt onion in oil; add tomato sauce, chile relish and salt. Cook until sauce is thick. Fry tortillas lightly in oil. On each put some chicken and cheese. Roll and arrange on hot platter. Over the top of the rolled tortillas, spread one wide strip of guacamole, one of sour cream and one of the sauce. Garnish with pickled onions or onion rings.

This recipe was taken from "Elena's Secrets of Mexican Cooking" by Elena Zelayeta. The green, white and red toppings give the effect of the Mexican flag. These are simple to make with leftover chicken and your own guacamole and very good.

Betsy Cosart   *Monache High School, Porterville*

Chicken in Nut Sauce

Serves 4 to 6

2 lbs. chicken breast halves
4½ cups cubed potatoes
2 tablespoons cooking oil
2 cups La Victoria Chili Dip

1 cup La Victoria Salsa Victoria
  (or milder salsa if preferred)
1 cup chicken broth
1 cup almonds, finely chopped
Ripe olives, sliced for garnish

In a large Dutch oven or oven-going skillet, brown chicken and potatoes in hot oil. Set aside. In a saucepan stir together Chili Dip, Salsa Victoria, chicken broth, and almonds. Bring mixture to boiling. Pour hot mixture over chicken and potatoes. Bake, covered, in a 375°F oven for 1 hour. Garnish with sliced ripe olives.

La Victoria Foods, Inc.   *City of Industry*

Chicken in Nut Sauce, page 90

Mexi-Skins, page 4

Quick Spanish Omelette, page 52

Seviche, page 100

Chile-Cheese Chicken Brea

Serves 8

4 whole chicken breasts
3 tablespoons butter
4 tablespoons sharp cheddar
  cheese, grated
2 tablespoons green chiles,
  chopped

1 teaspoon salt
1/4 cup butter, melted
1 cup saltines, crushe
1 tablespoon Dash seasoning
1/2 teaspoon chili powder
parmesan cheese, grated

Bone and skin chicken breasts. Cut down center. Flatten each half with a mallet. Mix together butter, sharp cheddar cheese, chiles, salt, Dash seasoning, and chili powder until well blended. Place a portion of the cheese mixture in each chicken breast and roll lengthwise. Dip each rolled portion into melted butter then cracker crumbs. Sprinkle with parmesan cheese. Spray baking casserole with Pam and place chicken breasts in casserole dish. Cover with waxed paper and cook in the microwave 10 to 12 minutes on HIGH. If desired, serve on a bed of lettuce and chopped tomatoes.

Mary Ann Mathews   Serra High School, San Diego

Chicken Mole

Serves 4

1 chicken, 2 1/2 to 3 lbs. cut up
1/4 cup butter or margarine
salt and pepper
1/4 cup onion, finely chopped
1/4 cup green pepper, finely chopped
2 small cloves garlic, minced
1 can (17 1/2 oz.) tomaotes, cut up
1/2 cup beef broth
2 teaspoons sugar

1/2 teaspoon chili powder
1/8 teaspoon ground cinnamon
1/8 teaspoon ground nutmeg
dash of ground cloves
dash of bottled hot pepper sauce
1/4 of a 1 oz. square unsweetened
  chocolate
2 tablespoons cold water
1 tablespoon cornstarch

In a large skillet, brown chicken slowly in butter. Season lightly with salt and pepper. Set chicken aside. In same skillet cook onion, green pepper, and garlic in butter remaining in pan until vegetables are tender. Add tomatoes, beef broth, sugar, chili powder, cinnamon, nutmeg, cloves, hot pepper sauce and chocolate. Add chicken, cover and reduce heat, cook till meat is tender, about 45 minutes. Remove chicken to a serving platter, keep warm.

Slowly blend cold water into cornstarch, stir into sauce, cook and stir till thickened and bubbly. Pour sauce over chicken.

Janette Brown   *Mt. Shasta High, Mt. Shasta*

Fiesta Chicken Kiev   (M)

Serves 4 to 8

4 whole chicken breasts,
  halved and boned
jalapeno pepper cheese, cut in strips
1/4 cup cheddar cheese crackers,
  crushed

1 1/2 tablespoons taco seasoning mix
shredded lettuce
diced tomatoes
sliced ripe olives

... each raw chicken piece with mallet between plastic wrap to flatten. ... ace portion of cheese on each piece. Roll up each piece of chicken, tucking in ends, to completely enclose cheese filling. Dip each roll in melted butter to cover then coat with mixture of cheese crackers and taco seasoning mix.

Arrange rolls in a 12 x 8 x 2 inch dish. Chill overnight or several hours, covered. Cover with waxed paper. Place dish in microwave and cook 10 to 12 minutes. Serve on a bed of shredded lettuce and diced tomatoes. Top with sliced olives.

Leftover Fiesta Chicken Kiev is good picnic food - slice when cold and serve cold. Cold slices also make good hearty hors d'oeuvres.

Jan Hirth   **Saddleback High School, Santa Ana**

Chicken Tacos

Serves 12

6 large chicken breasts	⅛ teaspoon pepper
6 cups water	⅛ teaspoon salt
1 tablespoon salt	½ teaspoon oregano
2 tablespoons butter	12 corn tortillas
½ cup onion	1 cup oil
1 green chile, chopped	¼ lb. cheese, grated
½ clove garlic	½ head lettuce, chopped
¼ cup cilantro	4 small tomatoes, chopped
2 small tomatoes, diced	2 tablespoons lemon juice
	½ cup avocado, diced

Place chicken, water and salt in a large pot and boil 25 minutes. Cool. Tear chicken into ½ inch strips and set aside. Saute butter, onion, chile, garlic, cilantro and tomatoes. Add chicken, pepper, salt, and oregano to saute mixture. Cook tortillas in oil, drain and add saute mixture. Top with cheese, lettuce, tomato, lemon juice and avocado.

Antoinette De Neve   **Jones Junior High School, Baldwin Park**

Chicken Mexi-Roma

Serves 4 to 6

1 frying chicken, or chicken parts cut up (i.e., breasts and thighs)	1 package Lawry's spaghetti sauce mix
2 tablespoons oil	1 large can (32 oz.) tomato juice
1 can (8 oz.) Ortega mild salsa	1 lb. spaghetti

Brown chicken in oil and drain remaining oil. Stir together remaining ingredients, saving ½ cup of tomato juice, and pour over chicken. Simmer until chicken is done (about 45 minutes) using extra tomato juice as needed to thin sauce. Serve with sauce over cooked spaghetti.

I have used this recipe for 20 years when I want something super easy and delicious. It cooks itself. A great Mexican-Italian combo. Other salsa's are good, but Ortega is the best. In our family it's known as "Chicken Come Catch Me" because it's a grabber!

Val Herford   **Sage Intermediate School, Palmdale**

Mexican Style Chicken Kiev

Serves 8

8 chicken breast halves,
  skinned and boned
1 can (7 oz.) green chiles, diced
4 oz. monterey jack cheese,
  cut in 8 strips
½ cup fine bread crumbs,
  dry (Panko)

¼ cup parmesan cheese, grated
1 tablespoon chili powder
½ teaspoon salt
¼ teaspoon ground cumin
¼ teaspoon black pepper
butter melted
tomato sauce

Pound chicken pieces to about ¼ inch thickness. Put about 2 tablespoons chiles and 1 jack cheese strip in center of each chicken piece. Roll up and tuck ends under. Combine bread crumbs, parmesan cheese, chili powder, salt, cumin and pepper. Dip each stuffed chicken in a shallow bowl containing 6 tablespoons of melted butter and roll in the crumb mixture. Place chicken rolls, seam side down, in an oblong baking dish and drizzle with a little melted butter. Cover and chill for 4 hours overnight. Bake, uncovered, at 400°F for 20 minutes or until done. Serve with either of the tomato sauces:

Picante Sauce

1 jar (16 oz.) PACE Picante Sauce, medium hot
½ cup hot water with 1 Knorr chicken bouillon cube dissolved
½ cup cold water with 1 heaping tablespoon of cornstarch dissolved

Tomato Sauce:

1 can (1 lb.) tomato sauce
½ teaspoon ground cumin
⅓ cup green onions, sliced

salt
pepper
hot pepper sauce to taste

Combine tomato sauce, cumin and green onions in a saucepan. Season to taste with the remaining ingredients. Heat well. Makes about 2 cups.

Lynn Robertson   **Esparto High School, Esparto**

Pollo Con Naranjas (Chicken With Oranges)

Serves 4

½ teaspooon cinnamon
¼ teaspoon ground cloves
2 cloves garlic, minced
salt and pepper
1 medium onion, minced
oil
1 large fryer, cut up

⅔ cup orange juice
pinch of saffron
2 tablespoons seedless white raisins
1 tablespoon capers
½ cup almonds, chopped
  or slivered
1 orange, sliced

Make a paste with cinnamon, cloves, garlic, salt and pepper, onions, and oil. Remove skin from chicken pieces and sprinkle and lightly rub with paste. Brown carefully in the broiler. Add orange juice, saffron, raisins and capers. If a lot of gravy is desired, add 1 cup water. Cover and cook in the oven until tender at 350°F for 35 to 45 minutes.

Add almonds and orange slices 5 minutes before serving. If desired, place under broiler a few mintues to toast almonds. Serve with a rice pilaf or spanish style rice.

Nan Paul   **Grant Middle School, Escondido**

Fiesta Chicken Ⓜ

Serves 8

4 whole chicken breasts, split,
skinned and boned
3 tablespoons butter or margarine
3 tablespoons Old English style
sharp cheese spread
2 teaspoons instant minced onion
1 teaspoon salt

1 teaspoon MSG
2 tablespoons green chiles,
chopped
¼ cup butter or margarine, melted
1 cup cheddar cheese crackers,
crushed
1½ teaspoon taco seasoning mix

Pound each raw chicken piece with mallet to flatten. In a small bowl, beat together 3 tablespoons butter and cheese spread until well blended. Mix in onion, salt, MSG and chiles. Place a portion of cheese mixture at one end of each chicken piece, dividing evenly. Roll up piece of chicken, tucking in ends to completely enclose filling. Fasten with toothpicks or twine. Dip each roll in melted butter to cover. Coat with mixture of crackers and taco seasoning mix. Arrange rolls in a 12 x 8 x 2 inch glass baking dish. Cover with waxed paper.

Microwave on high or full power for 8 to 10 minutes, rotating dish ½ turn every 4 minutes until done. Let stand 5 minutes before serving.

Dana Robinson   **South Middle School, Downey**

Chalupa

Serves 6 to 8

5 to 6 chicken breast halves, baked
12 corn tortillas, cut in quarters or eighths
1 lb. cheddar cheese, grated

Mix together:
1 can cream of mushroom soup
1 can cream of chicken soup
1 cup sour cream

⅔ cup milk
1 small onion, diced
1 small can Ortega chiles, diced

To bake chicken breasts, wrap in foil with a drugstore wrap and bake at 400°F for 1 hour. Cool, remove skin and cut chicken into bite sized pieces. Grease a large casserole or ramekins (individual baking dishes). Layer the ingredients, starting with tortillas, chicken, soup mixture and cheese. Bake, covered, at 350°F for 1½ hours. Take lid off casserole for last 15 minutes. This can be made ahead of time and refrigerated. Dark meat may be substituted instead of chicken breasts or both may be used. Leftover turkey may be substituted. This freezes well.

Judy McFerrin   **Reid High School, Long Beach**

Chicken Maria

Serves 5

2½ lbs. chicken pieces, skinned
1 teaspoon paprika
1 tablespoon butter or margarine
½ teaspoon crushed dried basil

½ cup white wine
¼ cup La Victoria Marinated Nacho
Sliced Jalapenos, rinsed & drained
¼ cup pitted ripe olives

Sprinkle chicken pieces with paprika; place in a shallow baking dish. Sprinkle on remaining ingredients. Bake, uncovered, in a 350°F oven for 1 hour, or till chicken is tender. Serve.

La Victoria Foods, Inc.   **City of Industry**

Fish Mexicano

Serves 4

1 pound red snapper or other firm
  fish
salt and pepper to taste
½ teaspoon garlic powder
½ teaspoon ground cumin
3 tablespoons fresh or dried
  cilantro, chopped

4 medium Anaheim chili, seeded,
  finely chopped
4 medium green onions with green
  tops, finely sliced
1 medium tomato, chopped
½ cup cheddar cheese, shredded
½ cup jack cheese, shredded

Sprinkle fish with salt and pepper to taste. Pat dry with paper towels. Layer fish in a single layer in a 9 inch square or round baking dish. Sprinkle with half the garlic powder, half the cumin and half the cilantro. Add mushrooms, chiles, green onions and tomato. Sprinkle with remaining garlic powder, cumin and cilantro. Bake at 350°F for 20 minutes. Combine the two cheeses together and sprinkle over fish. Return to oven and continue baking 5 to 10 minutes or until fish flakes easily with fork and cheese is melted. Note: There will be some liquid formed in the bottom of the dish that you can use like a sauce over the fish.

This is a colorful dish and low in calories.

Marianne Estes   **La Mirada High School, La Mirada**

Pescado Naranjado (Fish in Orange Juice)

Serves 6

2 lbs. fresh or frozen halibut steaks
  (or other fish)
½ cup onion, finely chopped
2 cloves garlic, minced
2 tablespoons oil
2 tablespoons snipped cilantro

1 teaspoon salt
⅛ teaspoon pepper
½ cup orange juice
1 tablespoon lemon juice
1 hard cooked egg, cut in wedges
paprika and orange slices for garnish

Arrange fish in oblong glass baking dish. In a small skillet, cook onion and garlic in oil until onion is tender but not brown. Stir in cilantro, salt and pepper. Spread mixture over fish. Combine orange juice, lemon juice, and pour over fish. Bake, covered, for 20 to 25 minutes at 400°F or until fish flakes easily with a fork. Arrange egg wedges on fish. Sprinkle with paprika and garnish with orange slices.

Sheryl Malone   **Poway High School, Poway**

Broiled Fish Louisiana

Serves 3 or 4

1½ lbs. fresh fish fillets
  (cut 1 inch thick)
⅓ cup La Victoria Salsa Brava
  Taco Sauce

2 green onions, sliced
1 medium tomato, chopped
Cilantro or parsley sprigs
lemon or lime slices

Arrange fish fillets on lightly oiled broiler pan; brush well with Salsa Brava. Broil 4 inches from heat for 3 minutes. Brush again with Salsa; sprinkle on onions and tomato. Broil 2 to 3 minutes more till fish flakes easily. Garnish with cilantro and lemon slices; serve.

La Victoria Foods, Inc.   **City of Industry**

Tuna Tacos

4 can (16 oz.) water packed tuna,
  drained
2 tablespoons vegetable oil
¼ to ½ cup onion, chopped
¼ to ½ cup bell pepper, chopped
2 cans (8 oz. each) whole stewed
  tomatoes or 2 whole fresh
  tomatoes, chopped
½ teaspoon cumin
½ teaspoon marjoram

2 teaspoons garlic powder or
  garlic salt or Lawry's Seasoning
1 teaspoon oregano
¼ to ½ teaspoon chili, crushed
2 teaspoons white vinegar
½ bunch cilantro, chopped
1 dozen corn tortillas
1 cup cheddar cheese, grated
shredded lettuce for garnish

Drain tuna. Heat oil in a saucepan and saute onion and bell pepper. Add tomatoes and tuna. Stir. Add spices, vinegar and cilantro and simmer for 30 minutes. Fill corn tortillas like you would a taco (3 tablespoons or more of filling), add some grated cheddar cheese on top of tuna mixture. Use and electric frying pan and heat oil to 375°F. Pour enough oil into the pan that the bottom is covered with oil. Fry taco on one side until brown then turn over using tongs. Cook on second side until brown. Drain tacos between 2 paper towels. Serve on a platter. Garnish with shredded lettuce. Serve with salsa, hot peppers, taco slice, black olives, etc.

This is a new version of the old favorite tacos. Thank you Amber Bolio for creating this recipe. Very unique.

Jennifer Gierman   **Ball Junior High School, Anaheim**

Prawns With Salsa

Serves 10

2 lbs. medium white shrimp in
  shells
1½ cups dry white wine
boiling water
2 garlic cloves, minced

1 teaspoon lemon juice
cilantro or parsley sprigs for
  garnish
La Victoria Red Taco Sauce
lemon wedges for garnish

In a large saucepan, cover shrimp with wine and water. Bring mixture to boiling. Add garlic, lemon, and a few sprigs cilantro or parsley. Cook 3 to 5 minutes or till shrimp turn pink. Drain shrimp; rinse well with cold water. Shell and devein shrimp.

To serve, arrange shrimp in a small dish with Red Taco sauce and lemon wedges. Garnish with cilantro.

Main Dish Variation:

10 cups hot cooked rice
Desired La Victoria Salsa, heated

Cook shrimp as directed above. Serve shrimp on a bed of white rice topped with warmed Salsa. Makes 10 servings.

La Victoria Foods, Inc.   **City of Industry**

Huachinango Veracruzano
(Red Snapper With Tomato Sauce, Olives and Potatoes)

Serves 6

6 medium new potatoes, peeled
  (about 2 lbs.) or use canned
12 medium fresh tomatoes, peeled,
  seeded and coarsely chopped,
  or substitute 4 cups drained,
  canned Italian plum tomatoes
1/4 cup olive oil
1 cup onions, coarsely chopped
1/4 teaspoon garlic, finely chopped
4 canned jalapeno chiles, rinsed in
  cold water, split, seeded and cut
  lengthwise into strips
  1/8 inch wide
1/4 cup pimento stuffed olives
1 tablespoon fresh lime juice
1/2 teaspoon sugar

1/8 teaspoon ground cinnamon
1/8 teaspoon ground cloves
1 teaspoon salt
1/8 teaspoon freshly ground black
  pepper
1/2 cup flour
6 red snapper fillets (about 2 1/2 to
  3 lbs.), or substitute any other
  firm white fish
4 to 6 tablespoons butter
3 slices homemade type white
  bread, trimmed of the crust
  and cut diagonally into 4
  triangles each
1 tablespoon fresh parsley,
  finely chopped

Preheat the oven to 250°F. Drop the potatoes into a large pan of rapidly boiling, lightly salted water, and boil them vigorously, uncovered, until they show no resistance when pierced with the tip of a small sharp knife. Be careful not to overcook them. Drain them thoroughly; place them in a baking dish, and cover them lightly with aluminum foil. Keep them warm in the oven while you prepare the other ingredients.

Place the tomatoes in the jar of an electric blender and blend them at high speed until they are reduced to a smooth puree. (To puree the tomatoes by hand, use the back of a large spoon to force them through a sieve set over a bowl, then discard any pulp and seeds left in the sieve.) Melt 2 tablespoons of the oil over moderate heat until a light haze forms about it. Add the onions and cook for about 5 minutes, stirring frequently, until they are transparent but not brown. Stir in the pureed tomatoes, garlic, chiles, olives, lime juice, sugar, cinnamon, cloves, salt and pepper, and cook over moderate heat for about 5 minutes. Remove the pan from the oven; cover and set aside.

Spread out the flour on a long strip of wax paper. Lightly salt each fish fillet, then dip it in the flour, coating both sides evenly. Vigorously shake each fillet to rid it of any excess flour. Set the fillets side by side on another sheet of wax paper. In a heavy 12 inch skillet, heat 2 tablespoons of the oil over high heat until a light haze forms about it. Add the fillets, three at a time, and fry them for about 2 minutes on each side, until they are golden brown. Add more oil to the pan when necessary. Transfer the browned fillets to a large heated serving platter; cover it loosely with foil and place it in the oven to keep warm. Quickly heat 4 tablespoons of the butter in another large skillet and when the foam subsides add the bread triangles. Fry them over moderate heat until they are browned on both sides, adding more of the butter if necessary. Drain the bread on paper towels.

To serve, remove the fish from the oven, pour the sauce over it (reheated, if it has cooled to much), and arrange the potatoes and toast triangles alternately around the fish. Sprinkle the fish with chopped parsley and serve.

From "Latin America Book — Time Life Series." This is one of my favorite company dishes for those who like spicy foods. You can tone down this dish by using fewer chiles.

Anne Dahl   **Ensign Middle School, Newport Beach**

Chupe de Marisco

(Baked Scallops in Cream and Cheese Sauce)

Serves 6

½ cup dry white wine
2 teaspoons shallots or onions,
    finely chopped
2 lbs. sea scallops, cut in half
    crosswise
2 tablespoons fresh bread crumbs
1½ cups light cream
6 tablespoons butter
6 tablespoons flour
1 tablespoon yellow chile paste,
    optional

¼ teaspoon paprika
¼ teaspoon ground nutmeg
¼ teaspoon cayenne pepper
1½ teaspoons salt
¼ teaspoon ground white pepper
1 cup plus 2 tablespoons Munster
    cheese, freshly grated
2 hard cooked eggs, quartered
    lengthwise
3 cups hot cooked rice, made from
    1 cup raw long-grain rice

In a large enameled saucepan or skillet, combine the wine and shallots or onions, and bring to a boil over high heat. Then reduce the heat to low heat for about 5 minutes, or until the scallops become firm and opaque. Drain the scallops and save cup of the cooking liquid. Set the scallops and liquid aside.

Preheat the oven to 350°F. In a small cup or bowl, soak the bread crumbs in 2 tablespoons of the cream. Melt the butter over moderate heat in a 2 to 3 quart saucepan. When the foam subsides, reduce the heat to low and stir in the flour, stirring constantly for a minute or two. Then slowly stir in the ½ cup of reserved cooking liquid and the remaining cream. Cook over high heat, stirring constantly with a whisk until the sauce thickens and comes to a boil. Add the soaked bread crumbs, chile paste, paprika, nutmeg, cayenne, salt and white pepper and stir until all the ingredients are well blended. Stir in ½ cup of the grated cheese and cook for a minute or two; then add the scallops, omitting any liquid they may have given off. Lightly butter the bottom and sides of a 2 quart baking dish or souffle dish, and arrange the hard cooked egg quarters on the bottom. Spoon in the scallop mixture and smooth the surface with a rubber spatula. Sprinkle the top with the remaining 2 tablespoons of grated cheese. Bake in the middle of the oven for 20 minutes, or until the mixture bubles and lightly browns on top. Serve at once from the baking dish accompanied by the hot cooked rice.

From "Time Life Book, Latin America." I use this recipe (without the rice and eggs) as a first course. It looks pretty served in scallop shells and is very tasty!

Anne Dahl   **Ensign Middle School, Newport Beach**

Red Snapper Veracruz Style

Serves 6

6 red snapper fillets, 1 1/2 lbs.
salt and pepper
1/2 to 1 cup flour
3 tablespoons olive oil
1 small onion, chopped
1 garlic clove, minced

1 tomato, chopped
1 tablespoons cilantro, fresh and
    chopped
6 oz. green chile sauce
12 oz. jack cheese
parsley

Dredge fillets in seasoned flour. Heat oil in skillet and saute fillets. Place in individual casserole dishes. In same skillet, saute onion, garlic and tomato for a few minutes. Add cilantro and desired amount of green chile sauce. Taste for seasoning and continue to simmer for a few minutes. Top each fillet with sauce and grated jack cheese.

Place in oven and bake until cheese melts at 350°F for about 12 minutes. Garnish with parsley and serve.

Maggie Aguirre   *Auburndale Junior High School, Corona*

Arroz Con Pescado (Rice With Fish)

Serves 6 to 8

2 lbs. white fish fillets, cut into
    serving size pieces
1 to 1 1/2 teaspoons paprika
4 tablespoons cooking oil
2 cups long grain rice, uncooked

1 medium onion, minced
1/2 cup La Victoria Salsa Picante
1 can (2.3 oz.) sliced ripe olives,
    drained
1/2 cup green onion, chopped

Sprinkle fish with paprika. Fry fish in oil till lightly browned; remove from pan. Add rice and onion to same skillet; brown till golden. Spoon rice, onion, and fish into a large shallow casserole. Add water to Salsa Picante to make 4 cups. Pour over rice. Cover and bake in a 350°F oven for 40 minutes or till water is absorbed. Stir in olives and green onions; bake 5 minutes more. Serve.

La Victoria Foods, Inc.   *City of Industry*

Foiled Fish

Serves 1

1 6 oz. fillet red snapper, cod,
    seabass, or orange roughy fillet
2 tablespoons La Victoria Green
    Chile Salsa

2 tablesoons tiny bay shrimp,
    cooked
5 sprigs fresh cilantro
Garnish: Lime wedges

Cut foil or parchment paper to fit fillet. Place fish on center of foil; top with salsa. Spoon shrimp over fish and top with 2 sprigs of the cilantro. Wrap "package", folding over edges to seal and form a packet. Perforate foil with fork; place on broiler pan. Bake in a 400°F oven for 8 to 12 minutes, depending on thickness of fish.

To serve, transfer packet to dinner plate. Cut open by slashing a large X into foil on top; fold back each segment. Garnish with lime wedges and remaining cilantro.

La Victoria Foods, Inc.   *City of Industry*

Linda's Seviche (fish marinated in Lime Juice)

1 lb. cubed firm white fish or shrimp or conch
1 cup lime juice (use lemon if lime isn't available)

Marinate overnight, turning frequently. The fish will turn white when it is fully "cooked."

The next day, add the following ingredients:

4 tablespoons oil
1 tablespoon vinegar
½ onion, chopped
2 tomatoes, chopped

¼ to ½ cup green chiles,
  chopped
salt and pepper
1 tablespoon oregano or
  cilantro. Try both one time

Chill for at least 2 hours. Serve over avocado slices or in small bowls.

Seviche is a loose recipe. You can use hot sauce or hot jalapeno peppers and change your spices and seafood for different tastes.

Anne Dahl   *Ensign Middle School, Newport Beach*

Seviche

Serves 8

1 lb. uncooked shelled, deveined
  shrimp, scallops, sole, and red
  snapper chunks
2 green onions, thinly sliced
6 to 8 cherry tomatoes, quartered
¼ cup drained La Victoria Nacho
  Sliced Jalapenos

1 teaspoon salad oil
½ cup La Victoria Salsa Suprema
½ cup lime juice
1 tablespoon fresh chilantro or
  parsley, chopped
¼ teaspoon dried oregano, crushed

Garnishes: lettuce leaves, sliced avocado, and orange, lemon or lime slices

In a nonmetal bowl, combine all ingredients except garnishes. Cover and refrigerate overnight. (The Salsa and lime juice "cook" the fish as it marinates.) To serve, drain Seviche and serve in small lettuce lined cups with desired garnishes.

La Victoria Foods, Inc.   *City of Industry*

Casseroles

Mexican Beef Hot Dish

Serves 6 to 8

½ lb. box mostaccioli
2 lbs. ground beef
1 large onion, chopped
1 clove garlic, minced
1 can (28 oz.) tomatoes, with liquid
1 can (6 oz.) tomato paste
1 can (6 oz.) water

1 can (4 oz.) green chiles, diced
1 tablespoon ground cumin
1 tablespoon paprika
⅛ teaspoon hot pepper sauce,
    (optional)
2 cups cheddar cheese, grated
1 cup corn chips

Prepare mostaccioli according to package directions. Drain. In a large skillet, brown ground beef, onion, green pepper and garlic. Drain off excess fat. Stir in tomatoes, paste, water, chiles, and seasonings. Simmer 15 minutes. Combine mostaccioli, meat sauce, and 1 cup of the cheese. Pour into a 3 quart casserole dish. Top with remaining cheese and corn chips. Bake at 350°F for 30 to 35 minutes. May serve with sour cream.

Rebecca Oppen Tice   **Dana Hills High School, Dana Point**

Corned Beef Hash Casserole   Ⓜ

Serves 4 to 6

1 can (16 oz.) corned beef hash
1 can (16 oz.) refried beans
2 chorizo sausages (about 6 oz.)
1 medium onion, chopped
1 can (8 oz.) tomato sauce

1 can (4 oz.) green chiles, chopped
¼ teaspoon oregano leaves
4 to 6 ozs. jack cheese, sliced
½ cup parmesan cheese, grated
tortilla chips

Spread hash in the bottom of a shallow 2 quart casserole, cover evenly with beans. Set aside.

In a frying pan over medium heat, cook sausage until crumbly. Stir in the onions and cook until limp. Drain well. Stir in tomato sauce, green chiles and oregano. Pour sauce over beans and hash. Top with jack cheese and sprinkle evenly with parmesan. Bake, uncovered, at 350°F for 30 minutes or until bubbly and heated through. Serve with tortilla chips for "scooping."

Though it may sound "un poco extrano," this is really good! With a green salad it makes a great dinner. Can also be heated in the microwave.

Maureen Tolson   **Lompoc Valley Middle School, Lompoc**

Enchilada Casserole

Serves 8 to 10

1 can cream of mushroom soup
1 can cream of chicken soup
1 can green chiles, optional
1 can taco sauce
1 soup can of milk

1 lb. ground beef
1 package tortillas, quartered
1 medium onion, chopped
1 lb. cheddar cheese, shredded

Mix together soups, chiles, taco sauce and milk. Brown ground beef. Put in a 9 x 13 inch pan in layers; 1st layer tortillas, then beef, onion, then cheese then soup mix. Repeat and bake for 1 hour at 350°F.

Vera K. Reed   **Hesperia Junior High School, Hesperia**

Beefy Mexican Lasagne

Serves 6 to 8

1 lb. ground beef
1 can (16 oz.) tomatoes, cut up
1 pkg. (1⅛ oz.) french fried onions
¼ cup salsa, optional
1 can (2.8 oz.) french fried onions
1 carton (12 oz.) cottage cheese

1½ cups chedder cheese, shredded
2 eggs, slightly beaten
12 flour tortillas
1 tomato, chopped
lettuce, shredded

Brown ground beef and drain off grease. Add canned tomatoes and taco seasoning (may add ¼ salsa for spice). Simmer **uncovered** for 5 minutes. Stir in ½ of the can of onions. In a bowl, combine cottage cheese, 1 cup cheddar cheese and eggs. Place 3 tortillas on bottom of greased (or Pammed) 8 x 12 inch baking dish. Overlap 6 tortillas around sides of dish. Spoon meat mixture evenly in dish. Top with 3 tortillas, then cheese mixture. Bake **covered** at 350°F for 45 minutes. Top casserole with remaining cheese and the other ½ can of onions. Bake **uncovered** 5 minutes more. Arrange tomatoes and lettuce around edge of casserole. Optional: add chopped onion, avocados and chiles.

This was given to me by a dear friend, Amber Bolio.

Marianne Traw   **Ball Junior High School, Anaheim**

Lasagne Mexicana   Ⓜ

Serves 4 to 6

1 lb. ground beef
1 medium onion, chopped
⅛ teaspoon garlic powder
1 can (1 lb.) tomatoes
1 can (8 oz.) tomato sauce
½ package taco seasoning mix
1 can (4½ oz.) ripe olives,
   chopped, (optional)
1 can (4 oz.) Ortega green chiles,
   diced, (optional)

½ lb. ricotta cheese*
1 egg
½ lb. mozzarella cheese, grated*
8 corn tortillas, cut in half
½ lb. mozzarella cheese, grated*

*Cottage cheese may be substituted
for ricotta and monterey jack may
be substituted for mozzarella

Place ground beef, onion, and garlic powder in a glass covered bowl. Microwave on HIGH for 3 to 4 minutes, stirring once at midpoint. Add the tomatoes, tomato sauce, taco seasoning, olives and chiles. Mix well. Microwave an additional 2 minutes on HIGH. Combine ricotta cheese and egg. Spread enough of the meat mixture in the bottom of a two quart rectangular ovenproof glass baking dish. Top with a layer of the tortillas, then ricotta and mozzarella cheese. Repeat until all ingredients are used up. Finish with meat sauce on top. Sprinkle top with grated cheese. Cover with plastic wrap and microwave on HIGH for 10 to 12 minutes, turning dish at midpoint. Let stand 5 to 10 minutes before cutting.

This dish combines the best of Italy and Mexico. Anyone who likes Mexican food and Italian lasagne, will love this. It is also much easier to prepare than Italian lasagne and much less of a mess to prepare.

Barbara Hansen   **Bishop Amat High School, La Puente**

Mexican Lasagne

Serves 8

1 lb. ground beef
1 package taco seasoning mix,
   (Lawry's)
1 can (8 oz.) tomato sauce
1 can (1 lb.) tomatoes
1 can (1 lb.) kidney beans, drained

½ lb. lasagne noodles
2 cups cottage cheese,
   OR ricotta cheese
3 cups cheddar cheese, shredded
olives, (optional)

Brown ground beef. Drain off fat. Add to ground beef, the taco seasoning, tomatoes, tomato sauce and the drained kidney beans. Simmer, uncovered, 20 minutes. Cook lasagne noodles according to package directions. Using a 8 x 13 inch rectangular pan, layer the noodles. It should make two layers with the sauce and shredded cheese on top. Garnish with olives, if desired. Bake at 375°F for 30 minutes, uncovered. Let stand 15 minutes before serving.

Susan Lefler   *Ramona Junior High School, Chino*

Southwestern Quiche

Serves 4 to 6

¾ cup cheddar cheese, grated
½ cup monterey jack cheese
9 inch pie crust, **unbaked**
3 large eggs, lightly beaten
1 teaspoon salt
¼ teaspoon white pepper

1½ cups half and half
1 can (4 oz.) green chiles, diced
1 can (2¼ oz.) ripe olives, diced
2 tablespoons green onions,
   finely chopped

Mix cheeses together and spread on bottom of pastry shell. In medium bowl, mix eggs, salt, pepper, cream, chiles, olives and onions. Pour over cheese covered pastry. Bake 40 to 45 minutes at 350°F, or until knife inserted off center comes out clean.

Can be served as an hors d'oeuvre or main dish.

Cheryl Pullan   *Terrace Hills Junior High School, Grand Terrace*

Mexicali Brunch Quiche

Serves 4

1 cup half and half
3 eggs, beaten
¼ teaspoon seasoned salt
⅛ teaspoon cumin

3 flour tortillas, medium size
1 cup jack cheese, grated
1 cup cheddar cheese, grated
4 oz. green chiles, chopped

Scald milk (heat in saucepan until small bubbles form around edge). Slowly stir milk into beaten eggs. Add spices to milk mixture and set aside. Press tortillas down into an ungresed pie pan. Edges will extend above rim and will be ruffled. Add grated cheeses and chiles, reserving some for the top. Pour milk mixture over cheeses and chiles. Sprinkle remaining cheese and chiles on top. Bake 30 to 35 minutes at 350°F until mixture is set. Cut into wedges and serve.

This is a great way to use up leftover flour tortillas.

JoAnne Bugh   *Hesperia High School, Hesperia*

Chicken Taco Pie

Serves 6 to 8

1½ lbs. chicken
1 large can enchilada sauce
1 can mushroom soup
1 large onion, chopped

½ teaspoon garlic salt
dash of pepper
1 bag (11 oz.) Fritos
1 cup cheddar cheese, grated

Boil chicken until tender — **reserve broth**. Remove bones and cut into bite size pieces. Combine chicken, enchilada sauce, mushroom soup, onion, garlic salt and pepper. Line a greased baking dish with half of the Fritos. Add chicken mixture, sprinkle with cheese. Cover with remaining Fritos. Add ½ cup of the broth. Bake at 350°F for 30 minutes.

Can use leftover turkey. Use only Fritos brand corn chips.

Vicki Giannetti   *Foothill High School, Sacramento*

Mom's Chicken and Burrito Casserole

Serves 6

5 chicken breasts
8 frozen burritos
1 can cream of mushroom soup
1 can cream of chicken soup

1 can olives, sliced
1 cup milk
¾ cup cheddar cheese, grated

Boil chicken. Remove skin and bones; slice meat into chunks. Place meat in the bottom of a 9 x 13 inch baking dish. Defrost burritos and slice each into 4 equal pieces. Place on top of chicken. In a separate dish, mix cream of mushroom soup, cream of chicken soup, olives, and 1 cup milk. Pour mixture over chicken and burritos. Sprinkle the top of the casserole with grated cheese. Cover and bake for 1 hour at 325°F. Uncover and bake remaining 20 to 30 minutes until hot and bubbling in the center.

Great main dish created by my Mom and loved by all who try it. Makes great leftovers if any remain after the first serving.

Katie Sheehan   *Warren High School, Downey*

Ole' Chicken Casserole

Serves 8

1 boiled chicken
1 large bag Doritos
1 medium onion, chopped
2 cups cheddar cheese, grated

1 can Mexican tomatoes
1 can chicken broth
salt
pepper

Boil chicken, remove from bones. Layer the first 5 ingredients in a medium casserole dish. Should get 2 to 3 layers of each ingredient. Pour can of chicken broth and salt and pepper to taste over the top. Pop into oven for 30 minutes at 350°F.

Garnish with whole Dorito chips and sliced olives.

Jolie Turk   *Dunsmuir High School, Dunsmuir*

Mexican Chicken Casserole with Flour Tortillas

Serves 4 to 6

1 dozen flour tortillas
1 can (4 oz.) Ortega green chile
  peppers, drained and diced
4 cups chicken, cooked and diced

1 can cream of mushroom soup
1 can cream of chicken soup
1 carton (8 oz.) sour cream
1 cup milk
1 lb. sharp cheddar cheese, grated

Cut tortillas into bite size pieces. Add chiles and chicken. Add soups and sour cream and mix well. Put in a casserole dish. Pour milk over the top and top with grated cheese. Bake in a 300°F oven for 1 hour.

This recipe was given to me by a former student.

Astrid Curfman   **Newcomb Junior High School, Long Beach**

Chicken Enchilada Casserole Ⓜ with Corn Tortillas

Serves 8 to 10

6 chicken breasts
2 small cans Ortega chiles,
  chopped
3 cans cream of chicken soup
2/3 cup milk

1 tablespoon chili powder
salt to taste
12 corn tortillas, shredded
3/4 lb. cheddar cheese, shredded
2 tablespoons green taco sauce

Poach chicken (or cook in microwave). Cool and shred. Make sauce of green chiles, soup, milk, chili powder and salt to taste. In a 13 x 9 inch pan, layer ½ of the tortillas, chicken, sauce, cheese and all of the taco sauce. Repeat, ending with cheese. Bake **covered** for 1 hour at 350°F.

Best when assembled 1 to 2 days ahead and then baked before serving.

Linda Hsieh   **Alhambra High School, Alhambra**

Chicken Tortilla Casserole

Serves 8

1 chicken, cooked
1 lb. mozzerella cheese, shredded
1 lb. cheddar cheese, shredded
1 dozen tortillas,
  cut in 1 inch pieces

Sauce:
1 can mushroom soup
1 can cream of chicken soup
1 can (7 oz.) green chile salsa
1 can chili
½ cup milk

Boil chicken until done. Put a small amount of chicken broth in the bottom of a 9 x 13 inch pan or casserole dish. Spread half of the tortillas on the bottom of the pan. Add layers of chicken pieces, cheese and the sauce. Repeat with the rest of the tortillas, chicken, cheese and sauce. Top with cheese. Bake at 325°F for 1 hour until hot.

Delicious served with fruit and a green salad.

Sandy Vickrey   **Winters High School, Winters**

Cal-Mex Dinner Casserole

Serves 4 to 6

1 package ready to bake biscuits	1 egg, beaten
1 lb. hamburger	1 cup sour cream
1 small onion, diced	1½ cups jack cheese, shredded
3 tablespoons taco seasoning	1 small can Ortega green chiles
1 teaspoon garlic powder	1 jar chile salsa
salt and pepper to taste	¼ cup olives, sliced
1 can (8 oz.) tomato sauce	1 cup cheddar cheese, shredded
1 can tomatoes, cut up	sliced avocados, optional

Press biscuits to form a layer in a casserole dish (lightly greased). Brown hamburger; add onions and cook until tender over medium heat. Add seasonings, tomato sauce and tomatoes; cook 5 minutes more. Mix together beaten egg, sour cream and jack cheese in a separate bowl. Add meat mixture; blend well. Stir in chiles, salsa, and olives. In casserole (biscuit) dish, add mixture, over dough. Top with shredded cheddar and place in oven. Bake for 30 minutes at 375°F. Add avocados, if desired, during last 10 minutes of baking time.

A spicy casserole using fresh California produce that will work as a main entree at dinner or lunch.

D. Yamamoto/Deanna Taylor

Mesa Verde High School
Citrus Heights

Chicken Tortilla Casserole

Serves 6 to 8

1 package (8 oz.) tortilla chips, slightly crushed
½ lb. monterey jack cheese, shredded
3 cans (12½ oz. each) chunk chicken

Sauce:

Combine the following and blend well:

3 tablespoons green onion, chopped	1 cup cream of chicken soup
½ cup milk	½ pint sour cream
1 cup (canned) mushrooms, drained	3 canned green chiles, chopped
	½ taspoon garlic salt
	½ cup black olives, chopped

Grease lightly a 3 quart casserole. Layer about ⅓ of the tortilla chips in bottom of dish. Place ⅓ of the shredded cheese over tortilla chips. Place ⅓ of the chicken over cheese layer. Pour ⅓ of the sauce over the chicken layer. Repeat layers of tortilla chips, shredded cheese, chicken and sauce two more times. Top off with the last ¼ of shredded cheese. Bake in 350°F oven, covered, for 40 minutes. Uncover and continue baking for 10 to 20 minutes or until cheese is melted and bubbly.

May garnish before serving with black olives and a few sliced green onion tops. This is a great dish for a buffet. It may be prepared a day ahead of time and refrigerated — add 10 minutes of baking time.

Geraldine E. Yeakel

Perris High School, Perris

Mexican Chicken Tortilla Casserole

Serves 6 to 8

1 to 2 to 2½ lbs. chicken
1 bay leaf
1 can cream of mushroom soup
1 package (8 to 10) flour tortillas
1 can Mexican-style stewed
   tomatoes with seasonings

½ small can jalapeno peppers,
   diced
12 oz. longhorn cheddar cheese,
   grated
1 large onion, chopped

In a large pan, stew chicken with bay leaf until tender. Debone chicken and cut into bite sized pieces. Lightly grease a 9 x 13 inch pan or a 2 quart casserole dish. You will be making three layers of all ingredients in the following order, ending with an extra layer of cheese: chicken, soup, tortillas, tomatoes/peppers mixed, cheese, onions. Bake for 1 hour at 350°F.

Mariane J. Simon　　　　　*Stanford Junior High School, Long Beach*

Los Feliz Casserole

Serves 8

8 oz. lasagne noodles
1 lb. ground round or ground beef
1 tablespoon butter
2 cans (8 oz. each) tomato sauce
8 oz. cream cheese
1 cup cottage cheese

½ cup dairy sour cream
⅓ cup green onion, chopped
¼ cup green peppers, chopped
2 tablespoons butter, melted
½ cup cheddar cheese, shredded

Cook noodles until tender and drain. Brown meat in butter; add tomato sauce and cook 10 minutes. Combine cream cheese, cottage cheese, sour cream, green onions, green peppers, and melted butter in a 2 quart casserole. Top with half the noodles; cover with cheese mixture, then remaining noodles, meat sauce. Top with the cheddar cheese. Cover with foil and bake at 350°F for 25 to 30 minutes.

This is a great recipe from the kitchen of Amber Bolio.

Marianne Traw　　　　　*Ball Junior High, Anaheim*

Stack

Serves 4 to 6

1 lb. lean ground beef
1 medium onion, chopped
2 tablespoons butter
2 teaspoons salt
¼ teaspoon pepper
2 tablespoons chili powder

1 small can ripe olives, chopped
1 can (16 oz.) tomato sauce
6 flour tortillas
2 cups sharp cheddar cheese,
   grated
⅔ cup water

Brown meat, drain off excess liquid or fat. Saute onion in butter. Combine seasonings, olives, tomato sauce, onions and meat; heat through. In a round 2 quart casserole, alternate layers of meat mixture, tortillas and cheese, saving ½ grated cheese for the top. Add water by pouring around edge. Cover casserole with lid or foil and bake 30 minutes at 400°F. Serve immediately, by cutting in wedges.

Norma Kerby　　　　　*Mt. Carmel High School, San Diego*

Layered Enchilada Pie

Serves 6

1 lb. ground beef
1 onion, chopped
½ teaspoon salt
1 tablespoon chili powder
1 can (8 oz.) tomato sauce

6 corn tortillas
1 can (4½ oz.) ripe olives, sliced
1½ cups sharp cheddar cheese,
   grated
1 cup water

Brown ground beef and onion. Add seasonings (salt and chili powder) and tomato sauce. In casserole dish, alternate layers of tortillas, meat sauce, olives and cheese. Add water, cover and bake in hot oven (400°F) for 20 minutes. Cut into wedges with a sharp knife.

Betty Hall   *Fallbrook Union High School, Fallbrook*

Mexican Egg and Cheese Bake

Serves 12

2 cans whole green chiles,
   seeds removed
8 corn tortillas
1½ lbs. cheese, about 6 cups
   (I use a mixture of jack and
   cheddar)
2 tomatoes, sliced and
   seeds removed

12 eggs
¾ cup milk
½ teaspoon salt
½ teaspoon cumin
¼ teaspoon garlic powder
¼ teaspoon onion salt
¼ teaspoon pepper
paprika

Line a well greased 13 x 9 x 2 inch pan with chiles. Cover with tortillas that have been torn into pieces. Spread with grated cheese. Top with tomatoes. Beat together eggs, milk and spices. Pour evenly over casserole. Sprinkle with paprika.

Bake, uncovered, for 40 minutes at 350°F or until set. Let stand 10 minutes before cutting for serving.

This dish is always the favored one at the breakfast my husband and I put on for his staff every December before winter break.

Martha Riediger   *Sequoia Junior High School, Simi Valley*

Fiesta Supper

Serves 4 to 5

½ lb. ground beef
½ medium onion
1 clove garlic
1 teaspoon salt
¼ teaspoon pepper
¾ teaspoon chili powder

½ cup ripe olives, chopped
1 can (4 oz.) tomato sauce
butter
6 corn tortillas
1 cup cheddar cheese, grated
⅓ cup water

Saute beef, onion, garlic. Add seasonings, olives, and tomato sauce. In a round 1 quart casserole dish, alternate layers of buttered tortillas, meat sauce and 1½ cups cheese. Sprinkle remaining ½ cup cheese on top tortilla. Pour water at edge into bottom of casserole; cover. Bake at 400°F for 30 minutes.

Nancy Martin   *Douglass Junior High School, Woodland*

Mexican Casserole Ⓜ

Serves 4 to 6

1 lb. ground beef
½ cup green pepper, chopped
½ cup onion, chopped
1 envelope (1¼ oz.) taco
  seasoning mix
1 can (8 oz.) tomato sauce
1 can (6 oz.) tomato paste
½ cup pitted olives, sliced

¼ cup water
½ teaspoon chili powder
1 cup sour cream
2 eggs
¼ teaspoon pepper
4 flour tortillas
2 cups broken corn chips
2 cups jack cheese, shredded

Crumble beef in a 2 quart casserole. Add green pepper and onions. Cook on high 3 to 5 minutes, until meat is brown and vegetables are tender. Stir and drain fat. Then add seasoning, tomato sauce and paste, olives, water and chili powder. Cook on low 10 to 12 minutes or until thickened. Blend sour cream, eggs and pepper together in a small bowl. Place two tortillas on bottom of a 12 x 18 inch dish. Top with half the meat mixture followed by half the sour cream mixture. Repeat layers. Sprinkle corn chips and cheese on top. Cook on low 10 to 12 minutes or until cheese melts. Rotate dish half way through cooking time. Let stand 5 minutes.

Good for compliments at a pot luck!

Jan Oliver   *Irvine High School, Irvine*

"Easy" Enchilada Casserole

Serves 8 to 10

12 corn tortillas
oil
1 lb. ground beef
1 onion, chopped
1 can (8 oz.) tomato sauce

1 can refried beans
¼ teaspoon salt
½ to 1 teaspoon chili powder
½ lb cheddar cheese, grated

Tear tortillas into pieces; brown in oil. Brown beef; add onions. Combine beef, onion, tomato sauce, refried beans and seasonings. Place a layer of tortillas in casserole dish. Add a layer of beef mixture. Repeat layers. Top with cheese. Bake for 30 minutes at 350°F.

Bonnie Landin   *Garden Grove High School, Garden Grove*

Enchilada Pie

Serves 6 to 8

1 dozen corn tortillas
1 small onion, chopped
1 lb. ground beef

1 lb. tillamook cheese
1 small can ripe olives, chopped
2 cans (10 oz. each) enchilada
  sauce

Brown chopped onion until tender. Add beef and brown until crumbly. Grate cheese. Mix cheese, meat, olives and sauce in a large bowl. Heat tortillas, one at a time in hot lard. Alternate tortilla and mixture in large casserole. Top with cheese and sauce and bake for 1 hour at 350°F.

Ginger Raven   *Chico Junior High, Chico*

Tijuana Torte

Serves 4 to 6

1 lb. ground beef
1 medium onion, chopped
1 can (16 oz.) stewed tomatoes
1 can (8 oz.) tomato sauce
1 can (4 oz.) green chiles, chopped

1 package Lawry's Taco Seasoning
 Mix
12 corn tortillas
1 lb. cheddar cheese, grated

Brown ground beef and onion in skillet. Drain off fat. Add tomatoes, tomato sauce, green chiles and taco seasoning mix. Mix and simmer 10 to 15 minutes. Place ¼ cup of meat mixture on bottom of a 9 x 13 inch baking dish. Place 2 tortillas side by side on meat mixture. Top each tortilla with some meat mixture and cheese. Repeat until each stack contains 6 tortillas layered with meat and cheese.

Bake in oven at 350°F for 20 to 25 minutes, until cheese is bubbly. Cut each stack (torte) into quarters with a sharp knife before serving.

This recipe is from Lawry's Patio Kitchens.

Amber Bradley   **El Capitan High School, Lakeside**

Supreme Nacho Casserole

2 cups refried beans
1 large onion, diced
1 lb. hamburger
1 can (4 oz.) Ortega chile peppers,
 diced

¾ cup salsa
3 cups cheddar cheese, grated
green onions
ripe olives
nacho chips

Spread beans in bottom of a 15 inch pan. Brown together onion and hamburger. Add peppers and salsa. Spread over bean mixture. Sprinkle cheese over meat mixture. Bake for 30 minutes at 350°F. Garnish with green onions and olives. Serve with nacho chips.

Brenda F. Hardt   **Maricopa High School, Maricopa**

Enchilada Casserole

Serves 6

1 large onion, diced
1 clove garlic, minced
2 lbs. ground beef
1 large can stewed tomatoes
1 tablespoon salt
½ cup oil
1 teaspoon chili powder

⅛ teaspoon cayenne pepper
1 can corn, drained
1 cup milk
2 eggs
2 cups yellow cornmeal
1 can black olives, pitted

Brown diced onion, minced garlic and 2 lbs. ground beef. Add and mix stewed tomatoes, 1 tablespoon salt, ½ cup oil, 1 teaspoon chili powder, ⅛ teaspoon cayenne pepper and drained corn. Mix together 1 cup milk, 2 slightly beaten eggs, and 2 cups cornmeal and add to meat mixture. Add olives and mix.

Bake in an uncovered casserole dish for 1 hour at 350°F. *Cover if it starts to get too brown.*

Cheryl Sakahara   **Piute School, Lancaster**

Enchilada Casserole

Serves 6 to 8

1 lb. ground beef
1 onion, chopped
1 clove garlic
2 cups tomato sauce
1 cup Las Palmas chile sauce
2 tablespoons vinegar

2 teaspoons chili powder
1 cup beef stock
8 corn tortillas
1 cup cheddar cheese, grated
1 small can black olives, chopped
oil for frying

Brown heat, onion and garlic. Add sauces, vinegar, chili powder, and beef stock; simmer. Brown tortilla shells in oil slightly. Alternate in a 9 x 13 x 2 inch casserole pan, beginning with tortillas, the meat mixture, tortillas, meat mixture, topped with cheese and olives. Bake at 375°F for 20 minutes.

Esther Siville   **Ventura High School, Ventura**

Enchilada Casserole

Serves 4 to 5

corn chips (6 oz. bag)
2 cups cheddar cheese, shredded
1 can (15 oz.) chili with beans
3/4 to 1 cup enchilada sauce

1 cup tomato sauce
1/2 teaspoon instant minced onion
1 cup sour cream

Reserve 1 cup of corn chips. Combine remaining chips with 1½ cups shredded cheese. Add can of chili, enchilada sauce, tomato sauce, minced onion and mix well. Pour into an 11 x 17 inch baking dish. Bake, uncovered for 30 minutes at 375°F. Spread top with sour cream, sprinkle with ½ cup shredded cheese and circle reserved corn chips around edge. Bake 5 minutes longer.

Sue Waterbury   **San Luis Obispo High School, San Luis Obispo**

Chicken Chalupas

Serves 6 to 8

2 lb. chicken breasts
1 small onion
2 cloves garlic
1 pint sour cream
salt
16 to 18 tortillas

oil
1 lb. cheddar cheese, grated
1/2 green pepper, sliced thin
1 can (4 oz.) roasted green chiles,
   diced
paprika

Cook chicken in salted water until tender. Remove from stock and pull chicken off bones into bite size pieces. Save stock. Grate onion and garlic into sour cream. Add a little salt and a little chicken stock to thin the cream slightly. Soften tortillas in hot oil, place on paper towels to drain. Wrap chicken and all but 1 cup of the cheese in tortillas. Place one layer of rolls in casserole dish; sprinkle with some of the green pepper and chiles, then spread with part of the sour cream mixture. Sprinkle with a little of the reserved cheese. Repeat layers until all ingredients are used, ending with sour cream. Sprinkle with paprika. Let stand at least 8 hours in refrigerator before baking. Bake at 350°F for 1 hour.

Jennifer Gierman   **Ball Junior High School, Anaheim**

Cheese Enchiladas

Makes 8 to 10

½ pound cheddar cheese
⅓ cup shortening

2 corn tortillas per person

Grate the cheese and set aside heat oven to 400°F. Melt the lard or shortening in a small frying pan over low to medium heat, NOT HIGH HEAT! Fry each tortilla in the hot fat. Use the tongs to hold on to the tortillas and fry about 5 seconds on each side. Stack on a plate.

Pour the cooled sauce into a pie pan. With very clean hands, dip one tortilla in the sauce and turn over once to coat both sides. Set on a plate. Place ¼ cup grated cheese in the center of the tortilla and roll up. Place open side down in a 9 x 13 inch pan. Repeat dipping, filling and rolling the remaining tortillas and place in pan. Pour any leftover sauce over the enchiladas in the pan. Do the same with cheese. Cover the pan with foil. Bake in preheated oven for 15 minutes.

Enchilada Sauce

¼ cup shortening
¼ cup flour
½ teaspoon salt

2 tablespoons chili powder
2 cups water

In a large saucepan, melt the shortening over **low** heat. Add the flour to the pan a little at a time and stir well with a wooden spoon as you add it. Stir until smooth. Add the salt, chili powder and water and stir well. Turn the heat to high and cook and stir constantly until the mixture comes to a boil. Reduce heat a little and cook and stir until the sauce has thickened, about 3 to 4 minutes. Remove from heat and allow to cool to room temperature.

Kathy Williams   *Jurupa Junior High, Riverside*

Acapulco Delight

Serves 8

2 lbs. lean ground beef
1 package taco seasoning mix
2 cans (7 oz. each) green chile
  salsa
8 to 10 corn tortillas
2 cups cheddar cheese, shredded

1 can (17 oz.) refried beans
2 cups sour cream
½ cup green onions, chopped
1 can (2.2 oz.) black olives, sliced
¼ cup parmesan cheese, grated
lettuce and tomatoes, chopped

Brown beef in skillet and drain excess fat. Stir in taco seasoning mix and water according to package directions. Add green chile salsa. Simmer 5 to 10 minutes.

Place 2 tortillas in bottom of a buttered 13 x 9 inch baking dish. Spread half of mixture over tortillas and sprinkle with ½ cup cheddar cheese. Top with 2 more tortillas. Spread with refried beans. Cover with about ⅔ of sour cream. Sprinkle with green onions and sliced olives.

Place remaining 2 tortillas over mixture and cover with remaining meat mixture and cheddar cheese. Sprinkle with parmesan cheese. Bake at 350°F for 20 to 30 minutes or until bubbly. Serve with chopped lettuce, tomatoes and remaining sour cream.

Lois Armstrong   *Sonora High School, La Habra*

Pastel Azteca

15 tortillas
oil
1 chili sauce recipe
1 chicken boiled with salt and
  pepper, boned and shredded

1 package (8 oz.) cheddar cheese
1 package (8 oz.) jack cheese
1 pint sour cream
1 can evaporated milk

Fry tortillas in oil lightly, not crisp. In a square pyrex, place 4 tortillas, spoon some sauce on top, then chicken, cheese, sour cream and evaporated milk. Make four layers the same. Cover and bake at 375°F for about one hour.

Chili Sauce

½ onion, chopped
2 fresh jalapenos (for a mild sauce)
2 tablespoons oil
2 cans of green tomato chile sauce
  (Herdez brand)
1 can (14½ oz.) stewed tomatoes,
  chopped

cilantro, chopped (about ½ bunch)
garlic salt to taste
pepper, pinch
marjoram, pinch
cumin, pinch
oregano, pinch
capful of vinegar

Fry onions and jalapenos in oil, add the 2 cans of green chile sauce, the chopped tomatoes, cilantro, spices and vinegar. Let simmer for about 15 minutes.

This is a great recipe from Amber Bolio.

Marianne Traw   **Ball Junior High School, Anaheim**

Mexican Beef Casserole

Serves 6 to 8

1½ lbs. ground beef
2 tablespoons oil
1 onion, chopped
1 cup tomatoes, chopped
or canned tomato sauce
⅓ cup chile sauce
salt and pepper to taste

12 corn tortillas, cut into quarters
½ cup red taco sauce
3 cups monterey jack cheese,
  shredded
2 cups sour cream
2 packages (10 oz. each) frozen
  chopped spinach, thawed and
  well drained

Brown beef. Pour off fat and remove beef, set aside. Add oil to skillet and saute onion until limp and golden. Return beef to skillet and add tomatoes, chile sauce, salt and pepper. Dip tortilla quarters in taco sauce, covering both sides. Cover bottom of a buttered 3 quart casserole with half the tortilla pieces, slightly overlapping. Spread beef mixture over tortillas, then sprinkle with 1½ cups cheese. Layer remaining tortilla pieces on top and spread with sour cream. Sprinkle on the spinach and top with remaining cheese. Bake, covered, for 30 minutes at 375°F. Uncover for the last 15 minutes of the baking.

If reheating, have casserole at room temperature and bake at 375°F, uncovered until hot and bubbly. Could be arranged in individual baking dishes.

Barbara Boling   **Orange High School, Orange**

Flautas

Serves 6 to 8

1 lb. ground beef
1 onion, chopped
1 teaspoon garlic powder
1 teaspoon chili powder
1 pint sour cream

1 jar green chile sauce
1 package guacamole mix
1 can green chiles, diced
1 package flour tortillas
grated cheese for topping

Fry meat and onions. Drain off excess grease and add seasonings. Stir in sour cream. Add 1 jar of green chili salsa and guacamole mix. Add can of diced chiles. Simmer for 5 to 10 minutes. Take a casserole dish and spread some sauce on the bottom. Take a flour tortilla, put some of the meat mixture on it and roll it up. Place the filled, rolled tortillas in the casserole close together. Pour leftover meat mixture over the top. Cover top with grated cheese. Cover cheese with chili dip.

If you want more sauce, after you place flautas in casserole, pour another jar of green chili salsa over the top then put on the grated cheese.

Karen A. Tilson   **Nogales High School, La Puente**

Tijuana Stack

Serves 6 to 8

1 lb. ground beef
1 medium onion, chopped
1 can (1 lb.) stewed tomatoes
1 can (8 oz.) tomato sauce

1 can (4 oz.) green chiles, diced
1 package taco seasoning mix
12 tortillas, cut in pieces
2 cups cheddar cheese, grated

Brown ground beef and onion in skillet. Add tomatoes, tomato sauce, green chiles, and taco seasoning mix. Combine thoroughly, and simmer for 10 to 15 minutes. Place ⅓ of the meat mixture in the bottom of a large shallow baking dish. Place half of the tortillas on the meat mixture. Top with an additional third of the meat mixture and 1 cup of cheese. Make another layered stack with the remaining tortillas, meat mixture and cheese. Bake in a moderate oven, 350°F, for 20 to 25 minutes or until cheese is bubbly.

Susan Roa Hope   **Lompoc Valley Middle School, Lompoc**

La Cocina Chiloquilas

Serves 6 to 8

1 medium onion, chopped
2 tablespoons oil
1 (1 lb. 12 oz.) canned tomatoes
1 package taco seasoning mix
½ teaspoon salt

2 oz. green chiles, diced
1 (6¼ oz.) tortilla chips
1 lb. jack cheese, grated
1 cup sour cream
½ cup cheddar cheese, grated

Saute onion in oil. Add tomatoes, taco seasoning mix, salt and chiles. Simmer for 15 minutes. Grease a 2 quart casserole; add ½ chips, ½ sauce, and ½ jack cheese. Repeat layers. Top with sour cream. Bake for 30 minutes at 325°F. Add cheddar cheese, and bake 10 minutes longer. Let stand for 15 minutes before serving.

Vicki Giannetti   **Foothill High School, Sacramento**

Patt's El Dorado Beef-Cheese Casserole

Serves 6 to 8

1 lb. lean ground beef
1 tablespoon instant minced onion
1/2 teaspoon garlic salt
2 cans (8 oz. each) tomato sauce
1 cup ripe (black) olives,
 ripe or sliced
1 cup sour cream

1 cup small curd cottage cheese
3 to 4 canned green chiles,
 seeded and chopped
1 package (6 1/2 oz.) crisp tortilla
 chips
2 cups (1 1/2 lb.) Monterey jack
 cheese, grated

Fry beef until pink disappears and is crumbly. Drain off fat. Add onion, garlic salt, tomato sauce, and olives to beef. Combine sour cream and cottage cheese with chiles. Crush tortilla chips slightly, reserving a few whole ones for garnish.

Place half of chips in bottom of well buttered 2 1/2 quart casserole. Add half of meat mixture; cover with half of sour cream mixture. Sprinkle with half of grated cheese. Repeat layers. Bake uncovered at 350°F for 30 to 35 minutes, or until bubbly. Garnish with reserved tortilla chips.

Cheryl Pullan   *Terrace Hills Junior High School, Grand Terrace*

Taco Casserole

Serves 8 to 10

1 large onion, chopped
1 1/2 to 2 lbs. ground beef
1 tablespoon margarine
1 teaspoon salt
2 cloves garlic, crushed
2 cans (8 oz. each) tomato sauce
2 tablespoons red **or**
 white wine vinegar
2 tablespoons chili powder, optional

1 can kidney beans, drained
1 package (10 oz.) tortilla chips
1/2 lb. sharp cheddar cheese,
 grated
2 cups lettuce, shredded
1 green onions, finely chopped
1 to 2 tomatoes, chopped
1/2 cup sour cream
1 small can ripe olives, chopped

In a large skillet, saute onions in butter until golden. Add ground beef and cook until crumbly. Discard grease. Add salt, crushed garlic, tomato sauce, vinegar and chili powder. Cover and simmer for 15 minutes. Add beans. Lightly grease a 2 1/2 quart or a 9 x 13 inch casserole dish and cover bottom with 1/3 of the chips. Sprinkle with 1/3 of cheese, then spoon over 1/2 of the meat mixture. Add another 1/3 of the cheese and 1/3 of chips, then add remaining meat sauce. Top with remaining cheese and chips. (This much can be done ahead; cover and refrigerate.) Mix lettuce with onions and tomatoes and sprinkle over hot casserole. Garnish with sour cream and sliced olives.

Pat Fiscus   *Sinoloa Junior High, Simi Valley*

Crunchy Taco Bake Ⓜ

Serves 4

1 lb. ground beef
2 tablespoons dried onion flakes
1 can (15 oz.) hot chili with beans
1 can (15 oz.) tomato sauce
1 can (6 oz.) tomato paste

1½ teaspoons chili powder
½ teaspoon salt
2 cups coarsely crushed corn
  chips, divided
1 cup shredded cheddar cheese

Crumble ground beef into a 2 quart casserole or medium bowl. Add onions. Microwave on High 4 to 6 minutes, or until meat is no longer pink, stirring to break apart after half the time. Drain. Stir in chili with beans, tomato sauce, tomato paste, chili powder and salt.

Microwave on High 6 to 8 minutes, or until heated and flavors are blended. Sprinkle 1 cup corn chips in an 8 x 8 inch baking dish. Spoon meat mixture over chips. Top with remaining corn chips. Sprinkle with cheese. Microwave on High 1 to 2 minutes or until cheese melts.

Joyce Grohman   *Bellflower High School, Bellflower*

Chile Relleno Puff Egg Casserole

Serves 4 to 6

6 eggs, separated
2 tablespoons flour
¼ teaspoon salt

dash pepper
1 can (4 oz.) green chiles, diced
½ lb. jack cheese, grated

Beat egg whites until soft peaks form. In a separate bowl, beat egg yolks, flour, salt and pepper until thick and creamy. Fold yolks into beaten whites. Spoon ⅓ egg mixture into a greased 1½ quart casserole. Pour in ½ chiles and ½ cheese. Repeat layer of egg, chiles and cheese. Top with remaining egg. Bake uncovered for 30 minutes at 350°F.

Great served with salsa, guacamole and sour cream.

Katie Morrison-Gold   *Olive Peirce Junior High School, Ramona*

Chiles Rellenos Casserole

Serves 4

1 cup half and half
2 eggs
⅓ cup flour
3 (4 oz.) cans green chiles, whole

½ lb. each - Monterey jack cheese
  and cheddar cheeses, grated
1 can (8 oz.) tomato sauce

Beat half and half with eggs and flour until smooth. Split chiles, rinse out seeds, and drain. Mix cheeses; reserve some for topping. Alternate layers of chiles, cheese, and egg mixture in a deep 1½ quart casserole dish. Pour tomato sauce over top and sprinkle with reserved cheese. Bake at 375°F for 1 hour.

This was served at a buffet which was served by a catering group. I had to have the recipe! Delicious!

Doris L. Oitzman   *Victor Valley High School, Victorville*

Chiles Rellenos Con Frijoles

Serves 8

1 lb. dried pinto beans
5 cups water
1 to 2 onions, medium
½ to 1 cup bacon drippings
1 can (15 oz.) California green
    chiles

1 lb. jack cheese
2 cloves garlic, minced
oil or butter
salt to taste
cumin to taste

Prepare refried beans. Combine beans in a pan with water and onions. Bring to a boil and remove from heat. (Or soak beans in cold water overnight). Return to heat; bring to a boil and simmer slowly until beans are tender (about 3 hours). Mash beans with a potato masher, and add bacon drippings. Mix well; continue cooking, stirring frequently, until beans are thickened and fat is absorbed. Cook onion and garlic in oil or butter until wilted. Add refried beans, seasoning with salt and cumin to taste.

Stuff each chile with a piece of cheese, about ½ inch wide, ½ inch thick and 1 inch shorter than the chile. Use about ½ of the cheese. Place a layer of refried beans in a baking dish. Add a layer of cheese stuffed chiles. Layer until all ingredients are used. Add the remainder of cheese which has been grated to the top of the mixture.

Dianne Sheats   *Gridley High School, Gridley*

Chile Rellenos

Serves 6

6 green chiles, whole
1 lb. jack cheese
½ cup flour
3 eggs, separated

3 tablespoons flour
salt to taste
pepper to taste
oil for frying

Drain and slice each chile lengthwise to remove seeds. Slice cheese and fill chile. Coat cheese-filled chile with flour. Beat egg whites until stiff. Beat yolks until creamy. Fold yolks into whites, adding 3 tablespoons flour and salt and pepper. Coat chile with batter and fry until golden brown — about 2 minutes. Serve with salsa.

Lura Staffanson   *Perris High School, Perris*

Chiles Rellenos Casserole

Serves 6 to 8

1 lb. cheddar cheese
1 lb. jack cheese
1 can (7 oz.) green chiles, whole
3½ cups milk

4 eggs
¾ cup flour
1½ teaspoon salt

Grate cheeses. Place ½ cheese in bottom of rectangular baking pan (9 x 13 x 2 inch). Split chiles open, remove seeds and drain on paper towels. Place on top of cheese in pan. Beat milk with eggs, flour and salt until smooth. Place remaining grated cheese on top of chiles. Pour egg and milk mixture over the top. Bake at 350°F for 1 hour or until set.

Ruth C. Findley   *Antelope Valley High School, Lancaster*

Chile Rellenos

Serves 6

6 California long green chiles, **or**
   1 can (8 oz.) whole green chiles
½ pound jack cheese
½ cup flour (to roll chiles)
4 eggs, separated

1 teaspoon salt
¼ cup flour
salad oil
1 jar Ortega Salsa

Prepare chiles, wash and cut off tips. Place on cookie sheet. Place under broiler. Using tongs, turn chile until blistered on all sides. Place chile into plastic bag and steam for 10 minutes. Remove the peel. Cut a slit in the side of the chile and remove seeds and veins. Chile is ready to use.

Stuff prepared chile with a piece of cheese, cut to fit. Roll chile in ½ cup flour to coat. Beat egg whites with salt until they hold stiff firm peaks. Beat yolks until thick. Fold yolks into whites and then fold in ¼ cup flour. Dip prepared chile into batter and fry in ¼ inch oil until brown on both sides. Place in baking dish. Top with Ortega Salsa and bake at 350°F for 15 minutes.

Debbie Scribner　　　　　　　　　*North Tahoe High School, Tahoe City*

Quick Chile Rellenos

Serves 8 to 10

1 lb. Monterey jack cheese, grated
1 lb. cheddar cheese, grated
2 cans (7 oz.) Ortega chiles

1 can (13 oz.) evaporated milk
6 eggs

Mix cheeses together. Slice chiles open and lay flat; remove seeds. Grease a 9 x 13 inch casserole dish. Layer cheese and chiles. (Cheese-chiles-cheese-chiles-cheese-chiles-cheese) (3 layers of chiles). Beat milk and eggs. Pour over cheese-chiles mixture in casserole. Bake for 45 minutes 350°F. Enjoy!

A very simple and quick Mexican dish. Very good - you won't have leftovers!

Pat Peck　　　　　　　　　*Cordova High School, Rancho Cordova*

Chile Relleno's Casserole

Serves 6

6 eggs, beaten
2 cups (24 oz.) cream style cottage cheese
¾ cup round crackers, finely crushed
1 can (4 oz.) green chiles drained, seeded and chopped
¾ cup (3 oz.) monterey jack cheese, shredded
¾ cup (3 oz.) cheddar cheese, shredded

Combine eggs, cottage cheese, cracker crumbs, chiles and half monterey jack and cheddar cheese. Turn into a 10 x 6 x 2 inch baking dish. Bake in 350°F oven for 45 minutes until set. Sprinkle with remaining cheeses. Bake 2 to 3 minutes more or until cheese melts. Let stand 5 mintues before serving.

Excellent casserole. Can be prepared ahead and baked when needed. Tastes just like chile rellenos!

Theresa M. Campbell　　　　　　　　　*Kennedy High School, La Palma*

Chile Rellenos With Sauce

Serves 4

2 cans (4 oz.) peeled green chiles
1/2 lb. Monterey jack cheese
  (approximate)
flour
3 eggs, separated
1 1/2 teaspoons cold water
peanut oil

Tomato Sauce

2 cups canned tomatoes, whole
2 large onions, finely chopped
1/2 cup peanut oil
1 teaspoon oregano, crushed
salt to taste

Cut chiles lengthwise, remove seeds. Wrap around a rectangluar piece of cheese to completely cover. Roll in flour; set aside. Beat egg whites and water until stiff; add egg yolks, continue beating until well blended. Dip floured cheese stuffed chiles into beaten egg and deep fry in peanut oil preheated to 350°F. Spoon hot oil over top of chiles and cook until golden brown. Drain on paper towels. Continue until all chiles are browned. Place in tomato sauce and simmer until heated through.

Tomato Sauce: Puree tomatoes in blender until smooth. In small skillet, saute onion until limp. Add tomatoes, oregano and salt to taste. Simmer covered for 10 minutes. Add chile rellenos.

Worth the time and effort.

Jan Pierre   *Cabrillo High School, Lompoc*

Chile Rellenos Casserole   Ⓜ

Serves 6

1 lb. ground beef
1/2 cup onion, chopped
1/2 teaspoon salt
1/4 teaspoon pepper
2 cans (4 oz. each) green chiles,
  cut in half crosswise and seeded

1 1/2 cups sharp cheddar cheese,
  grated
1/4 cup all purpose flour
1/2 teaspoon salt
4 eggs, beaten
1 1/2 cups milk
1/2 teaspoon tabasco, optional

Break ground beef in small chunks in a 1 1/2 quart casserole dish, combine with onion, salt and pepper. Cook, stirring several times to break meat up, for 5 to 6 minutes.

In a 7 x 11 inch baking dish, place half the chiles, sprinkle with cheese, top with meat mixture. Arrange remaining chiles over meat. In blender jar, combine flour, salt, eggs, milk and tabasco. Blend until smooth. Pour over meat-chile mixture and cook, 18 to 22 minutes, turning dish twice. After baking, let cool 5 to 10 minutes. Cut into squares to serve.

Merlina Phillips   *McCloud High School, McCloud*

Chile Bake

Serves 6 to 8

2 small cans green chiles
2 eggs, beaten
1/2 cup flour

1/4 teaspoon baking powder
1 cup sharp cheddar cheese, grated
1/2 cup milk

(continued next page)

Line bottom of a greased 8 inch pan with chiles. In bowl, mix eggs, flour, baking powder, cheese and milk. Spread mixture over chiles. Bake for 25 minutes at 325°F.

Quick & Easy!

Jan Pierre   *Cabrillo High School, Lompoc*

South-of-the Border Chile Casserole

Serves 4

butter	*¼ teaspoon salt*
1 package (3 oz.) cream cheese	*1 cup (8 oz.) can chili and beans*
¾ cup cottage cheese	*1 can (2¼ oz.) ripe olives, sliced*
½ cup sour cream	*2 cups corn chips, whole*
3 tablespoons green onion, minced	*½ cup corn chips, crushed*
2 tablespoons green chiles, diced	*½ cup cheddar cheese, grated*

Butter a 1½ quart casserole; set aside. Blend cream cheese until smooth. Add cottage cheese, sour cream, onion, green chiles and salt; mix well. Combine chili and beans with olives. Layer in buttered casserole, in order: 1 cup whole corn chips, chili and bean mixture, ½ cup crushed corn chips, cheese mixture, 1 cup whole corn chips. Bake for 25 minutes at 350°F.

Remove from oven; sprinkle with cheddar cheese. Bake 5 to 8 minutes longer or until cheese is melted.

I use this recipe from "Knudsen's Cooking for Compliments" in a Foods Lab. It is a favorite among students. (A delicious recipe featuring rich Mexican flavors!)

Mary Onderko   *Del Campo High School, Fair Oaks*

Green Chile Tortilla Casserole

Serves 8

1½ lbs. extra lean ground beef	*1 can (7 oz.) or (4 oz.) green chiles,*
1 large onion, chopped	*drained and diced*
1 can (15 oz.) chili beans	*1 lb. Monterey jack cheese, grated*
1 can (14½ oz.) stewed tomatoes	*1 dozen corn tortillas, cut in strips*
1 can (12 oz.) vacuum packed	*or pieces*
corn, drained	*1 can (4 oz.) black olives,*
1 package (1¾ oz.) dry chili	*drained and sliced*
seasoning mix	

Crumble and brown ground beef in a large saucepot. Add onions, chili beans, stewed tomatoes, tomato sauce, corn, seasoning mix and desired amount of green chiles. Bring to a boil. Reduce heat and simmer for 30 minutes, stirring occasionally. Lightly grease a 9 x 13 inch baking dish. Ladle some of the meat mixture into the bottom of the dish. Cover with a layer of tortilla pieces, then with a layer of cheese. Repeat layers until ingredients are used up, ending with the cheese on top. Sprinkle black olives over the top layer of cheese. Bake, uncovered, at 350°F for 1 hour.

Doris Bickel has made this a Career Center favorite at our school

Clyle Alt   *Bell Gardens High School, Bell Gardens*

Chile-Cheese Bake

Serves 8 to 12

10 eggs
1/4 cup flour
1 can (7 oz.) green chiles, diced

1 lb. Monterey jack cheese, grated
1 pint cottage cheese
1 cube (1/2 cup) margarine or butter

Mix first five ingredients together. Pour mixture into a 9 x 12 inch glass baking dish. Melt butter and pour over. Bake at 350°F for 45 minutes.

I got this recipe from a good friend, Becky. We have both served this often as a brunch main-dish; it is delicious with fresh fruit and your favorite bread or muffins. You can halve all ingredients and bake in an 11 x 7 baking dish. It tastes like a quiche without the calories of a crust.

Doris L. Oitzman   **Victor Valley High School, Victorville**

Casserole — Cheese Chile

Serves 2 to 4

butter
1 lb. cheddar cheese, grated
1 lb. jack cheese, grated

1 to 4 cans chiles, diced
4 eggs
1 can tomatoes, stewed

Butter a deep casserole. Make layers of cheese and add chiles. Separate eggs. Beat egg whites until stiff. Beat yolks. Fold whites into yolks. Gently pour eggs over cheese mixture. Bake for 1/2 hour at 325°F.
Add drained tomatoes, pushing them down with a fork. Bake another half hour. Serve hot.

Great for lunch!

Audrey Brown   **Loara High School, Anaheim**

Impossible Taco Pie

Serves 4 to 6

1 lb. ground beef
1/2 cup onions, chopped
1 package taco seasoning
1 can (4 oz.) green chiles,
    drained and chopped
1 1/2 cup plus 2 tablespoons milk
1 cup Bisquick baking mix

4 eggs
1 1/2 cups jack or cheddar cheese
    grated
sour cream
2 tomatoes, chopped
guacamole

Grease an 11 x 7 inch glass baking dish. Cook ground beef and onions until beef is brown; drain. Stir in seasoning mix. Spread in baking dish; spread with green chiles. Beat milk, baking mix and eggs until smooth (15 seconds in the blender on high speed). Pour over meat mixture. Bake for 25 minutes at 400°F. Top with cheese. Bake until knife inserted in center comes out clean, 8 to 10 minutes longer. Cool for 5 minutes. Cut into serving pieces. Serve with sour cream, guacamole, and chopped tomatoes.

I got this from Bisquick, and it is loved by everyone! So quick and easy!

Maryjane Dwyer   **Laguna Hills High School, Laguna Hills**

Foiled Fish, page 99

Mexicali Burger, page 77

Mexican Pizza, page 48

Chili Verde, page 79

Four Cheese Casserole

Serves 6 to 8

1 lb. ground beef
4 tablespoons onion, chopped
1 tablespoon garlic powder
1 can (8 oz.) tomato sauce
1 can (4 oz.) olives, sliced
1 cup IMO Dressing or sour cream

1 cup cottage cheese (small curd)
1 can (4 oz.) chiles, diced
1 package (7 oz.) tortilla chips
1 cup jack cheese
1 cup sharp cheddar cheese

Saute beef, onion and garlic powder. Add tomato sauce and olives and simmer for 5 minutes with lid on. Combine IMO with cottage cheese and chiles. Crush tortilla chips and grate the 2 cheeses. Layer 4 layers or make 8 layers using ½ of each. Bake for 30 minutes at 350°F.

High protein and great flavor.

Nikki Van Camp   **Poly High School, Riverside**

El Dorado Casserole

Serves 6

1 lb. lean ground beef
1 teaspoon minced onion
½ teaspoon garlic salt
2 cans tomato sauce
1 cup ripe olives, chopped

1 cup sour cream
1 cup cottage cheese
1 can (4 oz.) chiles, diced
1 package (6½ oz.) tortilla chips
2 cups (½ lb.) jack cheese, grated

Fry beef until pink disappears and is crumbly. Drain off fat. Add onions, garlic, tomato sauce and olives. Combine sour cream, cottage cheese and chiles. Crush tortilla chips slightly. Place ½ of the chips in the bottom of a buttered 2½ quart casserole and add ½ of the meat mixture. Sprinkle with cheese. Repeat layers. Bake uncovered for 30 to 35 minutes at 350°F or until done.

Marjorie Brown   **Cabrillo High School, Lompoc**

Mexicali One-Dish

Serves 4 to 6

butter
3 cups sour cream
2 cans (4 oz.) green chiles, diced
2 teaspoons worcestershire sauce

½ teaspoon salt
4 cups long grain rice, cooked
1 lb. monterey jack cheese, diced
½ to ¾ cup cheddar cheese, grated

Preheat oven to 300°F. Butter a 3 quart baking dish. Combine sour cream, chiles, worcestershire sauce and salt in large bowl. Spread ⅓ of rice in bottom of dish. Spread half of sour cream mixture evenly over the top and sprinkle with half of the jack cheese. Repeat layering, ending with remaining rice. Sprinkle top with cheddar cheese. Bake until cheese is melted and casserole is heated through, about 45 minutes. Serve immediately.

Add any leftover chicken, beef, turkey or tuna for variation.

Phyllis Kaylor   **Ray A. Kroc Middle School, San Diego**

Monterey Sunday Supper

Serves 8

1 cup white converted rice, cooked
1 can (7 oz.) green chiles, diced
1 lb. monterey jack cheese
3 medium zucchini, thinly sliced
1 large tomato, sliced
1 cup dairy sour cream

1 teaspoon garlic salt
salt and pepper to taste
2 tablespoons green pepper,
  chopped
2 tablespoons green onion,
  chopped
1 tablespoon parsley

Place rice in a 13 x 9 inch glass casserole, cover with a layer of chiles stuffed with cheese, zucchini, and sliced tomatoes. Mix sour cream with spices, green peppers and onions. Pour over vegetables. Grate remaining cheese over mixture. Sprinkle with parsley.

Sue Nall   *Temple City High School, Temple City*

Bean Burrito Bake

Serves 8

1 can (16 oz.) refried beans
1 cup biscuit mix
¼ cup water
1 lb. ground beef, browned and
  drained

1 cup thick salsa
1½ cups cheddar cheese, shredded
avocado, optional
½ cup sour cream

Mix well, beans, biscuit mix and water. Spread mixture in bottom and half way up sides of a greased 10 inch deep pie plate. Layer in order, ground beef, salsa and cheese. Bake for 30 minutes at 375°F. Cut into 8 slices. Top with avocado slice and a dollop of sour cream.

I served this dish for my son's 21st birthday party. It was a great hit. All of his college friends loved it!

Angie Garret   *Tenaya Middle School, Fresno*

Burrito Pie   Ⓜ

Serves 6

1 package (13 oz.) cream cheese
1 can (17 oz.) refried beans
1 egg, slightly beaten

2 tablespoons green chiles,
  chopped
4 flour tortillas, 9 inch diameter
3 cups cheddar cheese, shredded

Place cream cheese in medium glass bowl. Microwave at 50% (medium) 30 to 60 seconds, or until softened. Mix in beans, egg and green chiles. In a 9 inch round cake glass dish, layer 1 tortilla, scant ⅔ cup bean mixture and about ¾ cup cheddar cheese. Repeat 3 times ending with cheese. Microwave at 50% (medium) 10 to 15 minutes, or until heated, rotating every 3 minutes.

Joyce Grohmann   *Bellflower High School, Bellflower*

Frito's Tamale Pie

Serves 4

1 lb. ground round
1 medium onion, chopped fine
1 can (4 oz.) tomato sauce
1 can (4 oz.) water
1 can (16 oz.) cream style corn

1 can (10 oz.) Las Palmas red chile
  sauce
1 can (2¼ oz.) ripe olives, sliced
salt, pepper and garlic salt to taste
large bag of Fritos corn chips

Brown ground round and onion in skillet. Add rest of ingredients except corn chips. Lightly grease a 2 quart casserole dish. Layer corn chips in bottom of casserole, then a layer of meat mixture. Continue layers until chips and meat mixture are used. End with corn chip layer. Bake, covered, for 30 minutes at 350°F.

May be topped with grated cheddar cheese.

Betty Jo Smith   *Tahoe-Truckee High School, Truckee*

Tamale Pie Casserole

Serves 8 to 10

1 lb. ground beef
2 cloves garlic, chopped
1 onion, chopped
1 can (15 oz.) Gebhardt tamales
  with chili gravy, cut up
1 can whole kernel corn, drained

1 can cream style corn
1 can (8 oz.) tomato sauce
dash tabasco sauce
¼ teaspoon salt
1 can (8 oz.) black olives, sliced

Brown beef, garlic and onion, Mix other ingredients and bake in a 9 x 13 inch casserole for 1 hour at 350°F.

Roberta Priestley   *Alhambra High School, Alhambra*

Tamale Pie Squares

Serves 6

1 jar (14 oz.) spaghetti sauce
1½ lbs. ground beef
½ cup fine dry bread crumbs
¼ cup onion, chopped
1 egg, beaten
½ teaspoon pepper

1 package (10 to 12 oz.) corn
  muffin mix
1 can (4 oz.) green chiles,
  drained and chopped
½ cup monterey jack cheese,
  shredded

In a large bowl, combine ½ cup spaghetti sauce, ground beef, bread crumbs, onion, egg and pepper; mix well. In a 13 x 9 inch baking dish, pat ground beef mixture firmly into bottom of dish. Bake at 400°F for 10 minutes; spoon off fat. Meanwhile, prepare corn muffin mix according to package directions; stir in green chiles. On beef mixture, spread remaining spaghetti sauce, sprinkle with cheese. Evenly spread corn muffin mixture over all. Bake 15 minutes more or until golden brown.

This makes a good one dish meal. served with a salad.

Patricia N. Jones   *Norwalk High, Norwalk*

Claypot Tamale Pie

Serves 6

1½ lbs. beef sirloin, cubed
1 tablespoon oil
1 medium onion, chopped
1 teaspoon salt
¼ teaspoon pepper
1 clove garlic

1 teaspoon cayenne papper
¼ can (8 oz.) tomato sauce
¼ cup red wine
¼ cup parmesan cheese
4 green chiles (cooked and peeled)

Cornmeal crust:

1 cup yellow cornmeal
2 teaspoons salt
3 cups cold water

2 tablespoons butter
½ cup parmesan cheese

Brown beef in oil in skillet. Combine all ingredients (excepting cornmeal crust ingredients) in a wet clay pot. Stir cornmeal and salt into water. Bring to a boil, stirring often. Cook and stir until a thin gruel consistency. Reduce heat and simmer for 20 minutes. Stir in butter and cheese.

Cover casserole with cornmeal mixture. Place in oven (**do not preheat**). Bake 45 minutes at 350°F. Sprinkle with parmesan cheese and bake an additional 15 minutes.

Audrey Brown   **Loara High School, Anaheim**

Tamale Pie

Serves 4

1 can tomatoes
1 can corn
⅔ cup yellow cornmeal
1 lb. ground steak or hamburger
1 onion

1 bell pepper
¼ cup oil
1 teaspoon chili powder
olives (ripe)

Cook together in saucepan: tomatoes, corn, cornmeal. Cook 15 to 20 minutes. Stir often to keep from sticking. Fry ground steak, onion and pepper in ¼ cup oil. Add chili powder. Combine cornmeal mixture and meat mixture. Add olives. Bake in a casserole dish.

This was a recipe my mother made often when I was young.

Verna M. Buerge   **Turlock High School, Turlock**

Mary's Tamale Casserole

Serves 6 to 8

1 lb. ground beef
1 medium onion, diced
1 teaspoon chili powder
salt and pepper to taste

1 small can tomato paste
1 can tamales, drained and mashed
1 can whole kernel corn
parmesan cheese

Brown ground beef and onion; drain fat. Add seasonings and tomato paste. Mix tamales and corn in separate bowl. Layer mixtures alternately in greased casserole dish. Sprinkle with parmesan cheese. Bake for 30 minutes at 350°F. Garnish with ripe olives, if desired.

Mary Walter   **Mt. Carmel High School, San Diego**

Tamale Pie

Serves 12

2 lbs. hamburger
1 large onion, chopped
2 cloves garlic, chopped
2 cans (16 oz. each) tomatoes,
   chopped with juice
1 can (16 oz.) creamed corn
1/2 cube butter

1 1/2 cups milk
1 1/2 cups yellow cornmeal
1 tablespoon chili powder, or more
3 eggs, beaten
1 large can ripe black olives,
   coarsely chopped
salt and pepper to taste

Cook meat, onion, and garlic until done. Do not brown. Mix everything together and salt and pepper to taste. Pour into a deep 9 x 12 inch pan. Bake at 375°F for 1 1/2 hours.

Can make this up the day before. Store in the refrigerator and bake the next day.

Nancy Byrum　　　　　　　　**Patrick Henry High School, San Diego**

T.J. Tamale Pie

Serves 6

1 lb. ground beef
1 onion, chopped
1 can (16 oz.) tomatoes, cut up
1 can (14 oz.) kidney beans or
   pinto beans, drained and rinsed
1 small can whole kernel corn,
   drained

1/2 teaspoon seasoned salt
1/4 teaspoon pepper
2 teaspoons chili powder
1 small box cornbread mix
1 egg
1/2 cup milk

In a large skillet, brown ground beef with onion; drain excess fat. Add chopped tomatoes (with liquid from can), rinsed beans, and drained corn. Add all seasonings, mix well; cover and simmer 1/2 hour. Grease a 9 x 13 inch casserole dish. Pour meat mixture into casserole. Prepare cornbread as directed, using one egg and 1/2 cup milk. Spoon cornbread on top of meat mixture. Bake at 350°F for 20 to 25 minutes or until cornbread is golden brown. To serve, spoon onto individual plates and top cornbread with a pat of butter.

This is my husband's favorite . . . his mother taught me the recipe.

Joanne Bugh　　　　　　　　**Hesperia High School, Hesperia**

California Tamale Pie

Serves 6 to 8

3/4 cup yellow cornmeal
1 1/4 cups milk
1 egg, beaten
1 lb. lean ground beef
1 package chili seasoning mix
2 teaspoons seasoned salt

1 can (1 lb.) tomatoes
1 can (17 oz.) whole kernel corn,
   drained
1 can (7 1/2 oz.) ripe olives, drained
1 cup cheddar cheese, grated

Mix cornmeal, milk and egg in a 2 1/2 quart casserole. Brown meat in skillet. Add chili seasoning mix, salt, tomatoes, corn and olives and mix well. Stir into cornmeal mixture. Bake for 1 hour and 15 minutes at 350°F. Sprinkle cheese on top and bake until cheese melts (about 5 minutes).

This recipe is from the LA Times Culinary SOS Section, December 22, 1969

Lou Obermeyer　　　　　　　　**Loma Vista Intermediate, Riverside**

Desserts

Mexican Orange Candy

Yields 25 pieces

3 cups sugar
¼ cup boiling water
1 cup evaporated milk

¼ teaspoon salt
1 tablespoon orange peel, grated
1 teaspoon lemon peel, grated

In a large saucepan, melt 1 cup sugar over low heat until rich brown in color. Blend in boiling water; stir to dissolve sugar. Blend in evaporated milk. Add remaining sugar and salt. Bring to a boil. Cook, uncovered, over **low** heat. Stir occasionally, until mixture registers 236°F on candy thermometer. Cool to 110°F **without stirring**. Stir in orange peel and lemon peel. Beat until creamy.

Pour into an 8 x 8 inch pan. Let stand 4 to 6 hours to harden. Cut into squares.

Vicki Warner-Huggins   *Placer High School, Auburn*

Mexican Pecan Candy

1 slice bacon
2 cups brown sugar
1 cup white sugar

1 cup water
pinch of salt
1 cup pecans

Combine the bacon, brown sugar, water and salt in a saucepan and cook until hard ball forms in water. Remove bacon. Stir in pecans quickly and drop from spoon onto oiled cookie sheet.

Joy Nell Cain   *Willowood Junior High School, West Covina*

Nougat Candy (Mexico)

2½ cups brown sugar,
    firmly packed
1 cup sugar
2 tablespoons corn syrup

1 tablespoon butter
1 cup milk
½ cup chopped nuts
2 teaspoon vanilla

Combine sugars, syrup, butter and milk in a saucepan. Cook to soft-ball stage. Add nuts and vanilla. Allow to cool to lukewarm. Beat until creamy. Drop from spoon onto buttered dish.

Dorothy Wilson   *Dale Junior High School, Anaheim*

Pralines

Yields about 30

1 cup buttermilk
1 teaspoon soda
2 cups sugar

1 teaspoon vanilla
1 teaspoon butter
2 cups pecans

In an iron pan or very heavy pot mix buttermilk and soda, then dissolve sugar. Boil slowly to soft ball stage, 234 to 236°F. Mixture turns brown as it cooks and needs constant stirring. Remove from heat. Add butter, vanilla and pecans. Stir until it reaches sugar consistency or cream color. Drop in small cakes on waxed paper.

A very popular Mexican candy found in Texas.

Marsha Martin   *Auburndale Junior High School, Corona*

Mexican Wedding Cakes

Yields 3½ dozen

1 cup butter
¾ cup confectioners sugar
1 teaspoon vanilla

2 cups flour
2 cup walnuts, finely chopped

Cream butter, ¼ cup confectioners sugar and vanilla. With a spoon, blend in flour, gradually. Mix in walnuts. Shape into ¾ inch balls, rolling in palms. Place about ½ inch apart on ungreased cookie sheet. Bake in slow oven, 325°F for 30 minutes until light brown. Remove to wire rack. While still warm, roll or shake in additional confectioners sugar. Cool entirely. Roll in confectioners sugar again. Store in tightly covered container.

Bonnie McCormick   *El Camino High School, Oceanside*

Churros

Yields 1½ dozen

1 cup water
¼ teaspoon salt
1 teaspoon sugar
½ cup butter
1 cup flour

4 eggs
¼ teaspoon lemon extract
salad oil
powdered sugar

In a saucepan, combine water, salt, sugar and butter. Heat until butter melts. Bring to a full boil over high heat. Add flour all at once. Remove pan from heat. Beat mixture with spoon until smooth, clings together, and comes away from sides of the pan. Add eggs, one at a time; beat well after each egg until smooth and shiny. Stir in lemon extract and cool for 15 minutes (dough can be refrigerated here).

Fill a large pastry bag with large star on plain tip and fill with half the paste. Heat oil 1½ inches deep in a wide pan to 400°F. Start squeezing paste into oil until you have a ribbon of paste about 7 to 9 inches long. Cut it off with a small knife. Fry 2 to 3 at a time. Fry 5 to 7 minutes and drain on paper towels. Sprinkle with sugar.

Betty Getchell   *El Camino High School, Oceanside*

Mexican Mocha Balls

1 cup butter
½ cup granulated sugar
1 teaspoon vanilla
2 cups flour
¼ cup cocoa powder
1 teaspoon instant coffee powder

¼ teaspoon salt
1 cup walnuts, finely chopped
½ cup maraschino cherries,
  chopped
fine granulated sugar

Mix butter, granulated sugar and vanilla until light and fluffy. Thoroughly stir together flour, cocoa powder, and salt. Gradually beat into creamed mixture. Stir in walnuts and cherries. Chill dough 1 hour. Shape into 1 inch balls and place on a cookie sheet. Bake for 20 minutes at 325°F. Cool on rack. While still warm, but not hot, dust with fine granulated sugar.

Edith Novascone   *Burroughs High School, Ridgecrest*

Almendrado (Almond Pudding)

Serves 6

Ingredients for Puffs

1 envelope unflavored gelatin
¼ cup cold water
5 eggs (reserve yolks for
    custard sauce)

¾ cup sugar
½ teaspoon almond extract
¼ teaspoon lemon peel, grated
red and green food coloring

Sprinkle gelatin into cold water; let stand 5 minutes to soften, then place over hot water until dissolved. Separate eggs, placing whites in a large bowl. Reserve yolks for almond custard sauce (instructions for sauce follow). Add gelatin to egg whites. Beat whites with electric mixer at highest speed until they form a thick, white foam. Continue beating and add sugar; no more than 2 tablespoon per minute, sprinkling it gradually over whites. When whites form soft, curving peaks, add almond extract and lemon peel and beat in thoroughly. Tint ⅓ of the meringue pale pink with a few drops of red food coloring and tint another ⅓ of meringue pale green with a few drops of green food coloring. Pile pink, white and green meringue mixtures side by side in a shallow bowl and chill at least 2 hours or as long as 6 hours, with a cap of foil covering meringue without touching it. Spoon meringue into dessert bowls and pour almond custard sauce over each serving.

Almond Custard Sauce

5 egg yolks
¼ cup sugar
2 cups milk

¼ teaspoon lemon peel, grated
¼ teaspoon almond extract
¾ cup toasted slivered almonds

In the top of a double boiler, blend thoroughly 5 egg yolks, ¼ cup sugar, 2 cups milk and ¼ teaspoon grated lemon peel. Cook, stirring constantly over gently simmering water until mixture thickens enough to coat back of a metal spoon with a velvety layer. (If there is any evidence at all of graininess at any time, remove custard from heat at once and set in cold water, stirring to cool quickly.) Add ¼ teaspoon almond extract and ¾ cup toasted slivered almonds to custard, then set pan in cold water and stir to cool. Cover and chill (as long as overnight).

The Mexican people are known for their love of color and these colorful pink, white and green meringue puffs with yellow custard sauce are wonderful.

Myrna Orr   **McFadden Intermediate, Santa Ana**

Mary Anne's Instant Bunuelos

Serves "a Group"

½ cup oil
1 dozen flour tortillas

1 cup sugar
1½ tablespoons cinnamon

Heat oil to 375°F. Fry tortillas until brown on both sides. Drain on paper towels. Combine sugar and cinnamon and sprinkle on both sides of tortillas. Serve.

Reiko Ikkanda   **South Pasadena High School, South Pasadena**

Bread Pudding

Serves 6

5 slices firm white bread
3 eggs, slightly beaten
1 teaspoon vanilla

½ teaspoon cinnamon
½ cup sugar
milk
nuts and raisins

Break bread apart into small pieces. In a bowl beat eggs, vanilla, cinnamon, and sugar. Add the bread to egg mixture. Pour in enough milk to soak up the bread and mix well. Add desired amount of nuts and raisins and stir. Pour into baking dish and bake at 350 degrees for 45 minutes or until knife inserted half way between center and edge comes out clean.

This recipe has been prepared by my mother since I was a child, and a real favorite in our household.

Gerry Henderson   **Temple City High School, Temple City**

Margarita Pie

Serves 6

Pretzel crumb crust:

5 tablespoons butter
3 tablespoons sugar

1 cup each pretzel crumbs and
   vanilla wafer crumbs

Melt butter in a 9 inch pie plate. Add sugar and crumbs, mix well. Reserve 1 tablespoon for garnish; press remaining mixture into bottom and sides of pie plate.

Margarita Cocktail filling:

1 envelope unflavored gelatin
1 teaspoon lemon peel, grated
7 tablespoons freshly squeezed
   lemon juice
5 egg yolks
½ cup sugar
¼ teaspoon salt

5 tablespoons tequilla
2 tablespoons plus 2 teaspoons
   triple sec
5 egg whites
7 tablespoons sugar
1 lemon unpeeled, thinly cut
   into cartwheels

Soften gelatin in mixture of lemon peel and juice on low heat for approximately 2 minutes. Beat egg yolks until very thick; beat in ½ cup sugar and salt. Add to gelatin mixture and cook until slightly thickened. Stir and add liquors. Chill over ice water or in refrigerator, stirring frequently until cool (mixture should not be too thick). Beat egg whites to soft peak stage; gradually beat in 7 tablespoons sugar at high speed until all sugar is used. Whites should be glossy and moist and tips of peaks should fall over slightly.

Carefully fold yolk mixture into whites. Spoon into chilled pretzel crust; sprinkle with reserved crumbs. Prepare lemon slices for twists; arrange around edge of pie. Chill until firm.

Serve pie the same day it is made.

Susan Lingenfelter   **Edgewood High School, West Covina**

Avocado Pie

Serves 8

Crust:

24 graham crackers
2 to 3 tablespoons sugar
1 cube butter, melted

dash of salt
dash of cinnamon

Roll out graham crackers to crush. Add remaining ingredients and mix well. Line pie plate by pressing mixture against edges and bottom. Save enough of the mixture for topping.

Filling:

1 can sweetened condensed
  eagle brand milk
2/3 cup sieved avocado

1/2 cup lemon juice
2 egg yolks
dash of salt

Mix all ingredients well. Pour into prepared graham cracker crust. Sprinkle remainder of graham cracker crumbs on top. Bake at 350°F for 15 minutes.

Gerry Henderson   *Temple City High School, Temple City*

Bananas Mexicana   Ⓜ

Serves 4

2 tablespoons butter or margarine
1/4 cup brown sugar
1/4 cup orange juice

1/4 teaspoon ground cinnamon
2 bananas, peeled and sliced
4 scoops ice cream

Melt margarine in a small skillet with brown sugar, orange juice, and cinnamon. Cook over medium heat until sugar dissolves. Add banana slices. Stir and cook over medium heat just to heat bananas through. Pour bananas and sauce over ice cream. Serve immediately.

The sauce can also be prepared in the microwave by using a Pyrex casserole or large Pyrex measuring cup in place of the skillet. Microwave — HIGH setting for 2 minutes or until sugar is dissolved and 30 to 55 seconds until bananas are heated. Original recipe sent to Home Ec teachers by Olive Industry.

Joe Ann Gatley   *Rogers Junior High, Long Beach*

Spanish Flan

Serves 8

8 eggs
2/3 cup granulated sugar
1/4 teaspoon salt
2 cans (14 oz.) evaporated milk

2 tablespoons vanilla extract
1 tablespoon brandy
1/2 cup light brown sugar, packed

Preheat oven to 350°F. Beat eggs until yolks and whites are well blended. Add granulated sugar and salt and mix well. Beat in milk and add the vanilla and brandy. Sift the brown sugar into bottom of loaf pan and pour custard over it gently. Place in shallow baking pan with hot water. Bake for approximately 1 hour. Do not cover. Refrigerate overnight.

Yvonne Lindrum   *Schurr High School, Montebello*

Mango Dessert

Serves 4 to 6

1 can (about 20 oz.) mangos
1 jigger unflavored brandy
3 packages (about 3 oz. each)
  lady fingers

1 pint whipping cream
sugar to taste
½ teaspoon vanilla
1 cup pecans

Open canned mangos, reserving fruit syrup. Chop mangos into small pieces. Return fruit to syrup. Add 1 jigger of brandy to syrup. Open packages of lady fingers. Dunk lady fingers into fruit syrup quickly one-by-one and line the bottom and sides of a 2 quart glass pan. Add a layer of chopped mangos. Beat sugar and vanilla with whipped cream. Top with layer of sweetened whipped cream and chopped pecans. Alternate layers of lady fingers, mangos, whipped cream and pecans, ending with whipped cream. Garnish with pecan halves. Refrigerate 3 to 4 hours. Cut in squares to serve. **Note:** frozen strawberries or canned freestone peaches may be substituted for mangos.

This comes from my sister-in-law, Lora Ortega McCracken, in Mexico City.

Judy Stinton   **Mt. Miguel High School, Spring Valley**

Fried Ice Cream

Serves 4

4 vanilla ice cream balls
1 cup corn flakes
pancake batter

powdered sugar
honey

Form 4 balls from ice cream. Roll in uncrushed corn flakes and place on a cookie sheet. Freeze for 24 hours. Prepare pancake batter, reduce the amount of liquid to make a thicker batter. Roll ice cream balls in the batter and return to the freezer at once. Make sure the ice cream is completely covered. Freeze at least 4 more hours.

Heat oil in a deep fat cooker, to 400°F. Carefully put each ball into the cooker. Cook until golden brown (about 30 seconds). Remove from oil. Serve at once with powdered sugar or warmed honey.

Audrey Rogers   **Placer High School, Auburn**

Watermelon-Lemonade Ice

Yields 1½ pints of "Melonade"

2 cups sieved watermelon pulp (put in blender)
2 egg whites (stiffly beaten)
1 small can frozen lemonade concentrate (thawed)
1 lemonade can of water

Combine watermelon pulp, lemonade and water. Pour into freezing tray. Freeze until mushy. Place in chilled bowls; add egg whites; mix thoroughly. Return to tray. Freeze until firm, stirring once or twice during freezing.

Joy Nell Cain   **Willowood Junior High School, West Covina**

Mexican Wedding Cakes

Yields approximately 30

1 cup butter, softened
¾ cup confectioners sugar
2 teaspoons vanilla
1 tablespoon water
2 cups flour
1 cup walnuts, finely chopped
confectioners sugar

In a large bowl, cream butter and powdered sugar. Stir in vanilla and a tablespoon of water. In another bowl, mix flour and nuts together. Add to butter mixture. Shape into small balls. Place on ungreased cookie sheet and bake for 20 minutes in 300°F oven. Roll in powdered sugar.

These little wedding cakes were traditionally served at Mexican wedding receptions but now at parties, church gatherings, etc.

Jan Oliver   *Irvine High School, Irvine*

INDEX

APPETIZERS, SALSAS, BEVERAGES

APPETIZERS, SALSAS, BEVERAGES (continued)

BREADS

CASSEROLES

CASSEROLES (continued)

DESSERTS

MAIN DISHES (BEEF AND PORK)

MAIN DISHES (Beef and Pork) (continued)

Meat Loaf Suprema 62
Mexicali Burger 77
Mexicali Meatballs 62
Mexican Beefies 57
Mexican Meat Mix 70
Mexican Monte Carlo Sandwich 79
Mexican Pepper Steak 60
Mexican Pile-On 75
Mexican Pizza 77
Mexican Pot Roast 61
Mexican Stir-Fry 74
Picadillo (Mexican Hash) 71
Quick Chorizo Quiche 79
Quick and Easy Burritos 72
Shredded Beef Burritos 72
Sour Cream Enchiladas 70,71
Steak Tacos with Guacamole 58
Stir Fry South of the Border 63
Super Supper Nachos 76
Supper Nachos 75,77
Tijuana Pie 74
Tostadas Sonorenses 82

MAIN DISHES (Poultry and Seafood)

Arroz Con Pescado 99
Broiled Fish Louisiana 95
Chalupa 94
mmm ... Chicken Enchiladas 89
Chicken Enchiladas in Cheese Cream 86
Chicken in Nut Sauce 90
Chicken Maria 94
Chicken Mexi-Roma 92
Chicken Mole 91
Chicken or Beef Enchiladas 85
Chicken Sour Cream Enchilada 85
Chicken Tacos 92
Chile-Cheese Chicken Breasts 91
Chupe de Marisco 98
"Coach Yancey's Favorite Dish" 85
Fiesta Chicken 94
Fiesta Chicken Kiev 115
Fish Mexicano 95
Foiled Fish 99
Huachinango Veracruzano 97
Linda's Seviche 100
Mexican Chicken Rollups (Crescent Style) 89
Mexican Roll-ups 87
Mexican Style Chicken Kiev 93
Pescado Naranjado 95
Pollo Con Naranjas 93

MAIN ENTREES *(Poultry and Seafood) (Continued)*

SALADS

SOUPS

VEGETABLES

VEGETABLES (continued)

RECIPES FOR PHOTO PAGES

Alphabetized Contributors List

AAA

Aguirre, Maggie, 3, 7, 99
Auburndale JHS
Corona

Alt, Clyle, 21, 88, 121
Bell Gardens HS
Bell Gardens

Anderson, Ramona, 28, 29
Mira Mesa HS
San Diego

Armstrong, Lois, 44, 113
Sonora HS
La Habra

BBB

Baczynski, Kathie, 65
Mt. Carmel HS
San Diego

Baldiviez, Mary Ann, 81
El Camino JHS
Santa Maria

Bass, Alcyone, 17
Hamilton JHS
Long Beach

Behrends, Barbara, 86
Mojave HS
Mojave

Bennett, Karen, 5, 20
Valencia HS
Placentia

Benson, Elda G., 8
Corona JHS
Corona

Black-Eacker, Ellen, 78
Nogales, HS
La Puente

Blough, Shirley, 16
Hillside JHS
Simi Valley

Boling, Barbara, 54, 55, 83, 114
Orange HS
Orange

Bradley, Amber, 4, 111
El Capitan HS
Lakeside

Braxton, Linda, 59
Grace Davis HS
Modesto

Bressler, Barbara, 14
Buena Park HS
Buena Park

Brown, Audrey, 63, 122, 126
Loara HS
Anaheim

Brown, Darlene, 87
Golden Valley Int. School
San Bernardino

Brown, Janette, 91
Mt. Shasta HS
Mt. Shasta

Brown, Marjorie, 123
Cabrillo HS
Lompoc

Brown, Marlene
La Victoria Foods, Inc.
City of Industry
4, 8, 17, 26, 28, 34, 35, 44, 48,
52, 54, 60, 61, 62, 77, 79, 82, 90,
94, 95, 96, 99, 100

Buerge, Verna, 68, 126
Turlock HS
Turlock

Bugh, JoAnne, 104, 127
Hesperia HS
Hesperia

Burke, Brenda, 17, 46, 49
Mt. Whitney HS
Visalia

Burns, Jeannie, 45, 71
Los Osos JHS
Los Osos

Byrum, Nancy, 20, 127
Patrick Henry HS
San Diego

CCC

Cain, Joy Nell, 129, 134
Willowood JHS
West Covina

Campbell, Theresa M. 119
Kennedy HS
La Palma

Chutuk, Phyllis, 77
Oceanside HS
Oceanside

Cornwall, Judy, 7
Poly HS
Long Beach

Cosart, Betsy, 43, 71, 90
Monache HS
Porterville

Crawford, Kathy, 71
Thompson JHS
Bakersfield

Cronkhite, Mary, 10
Antelope Valley HS
Lancaster

Curfman, Astrid, 106
Newcomb JHS
Long Beach

DDD

Dahl, Anne, 3, 44, 97, 98, 100
Ensign Mid. School
Newport Beach

Delap, Carole, 80
Golden West HS
Visalia

DeNeve, Antoinette, 10, 60, 92
Jones JHS
Baldwin Park

Dempsey, Jean, 72
Santa Paula HS
Santa Paula

Dwyer, Maryjane, 122
Laguna Hills HS
Laguna Hills

Dyle, Patricia, 53
Kennedy HS
La Palma

EEE

Earnest, Nancy, 62
Victor Valley HS
Victorville

Enyeart, Mary Jo, 16
South Mid. School
Downey

Estes, Marianne, 95
La Mirada HS
La Mirada

FFF

Fial, Joanne, 5, 15, 90
East Mid. School
Downey

Fielding, Madelyn V., 23
Jordan HS
Long Beach

Findley, Ruth C.,118
Antelope Valley HS
Lancaster

Fiscus, Pat, 10, 116
Sinaloa JHS
Simi Valley

Forbes, Roberta, 5
Marshall JHS
Long Beach

Ford, Barbara, 32
Cope JHS
Redlands

Ford, Pam, 80
Temecula Valley HS
Rancho California

Fox, Sydney, 39, 40, 53, 58
Orange Glen HS
Escondido

Fuller, Glennell, 13
Glendora HS
Glendora

GGG

Garrett, Angie, 40, 124
Tenaya Mid. School
Fresno

Gatley, Joe Ann, 133
Rogers JHS
Long Beach

Getchell, Betty, 130
El Camino HS
Oceanside

Giannetti, Vicki, 49, 105, 115
Foothill HS
Sacramento

Gierman, Jennifer, 9, 96, 112
Ball JHS
Anaheim

Goble, Donna, 67
Almondale School
Little Rock

Golden, Elaine, 22
Rancho-Starbuck JHS
Whittier

Goughnour, Kelly, 72
Yreka HS
Yreka

Grohman, Joyce,
29, 31, 35, 117, 124
Bellflower HS
Bellflower

HHH

Hall, Betty, 109
Fallbrook Union HS
Fallbrook

Hampton, Julie, 8
Franklin JHS
Long Beach

Hansen, Barbara, 21, 103
Bishop Amat HS
La Puente

Hardt, Brenda F., 111
Maricopa HS
Maricopa

Henderson, Gerry, 132, 133
Temple City HS
Temple City

Henry, Claudia L., 52
Colfax HS
Colfax

Herford, Val, 92
Sage Int. School
Palmdale

Herman, April, 25, 66
Townsend JHS
Chino

Hill, Leota, 33
Saddleback HS
Santa Ana

Hirth, Jan, 91
Saddleback HS
Santa Ana

Hobberlin, Nancy, 55
Arroyo Grande HS
Arroyo Grande

Hope, Susan Roa, 20, 45, 115
Lompoc Valley Mid. School
Lompoc

Hsieh, Linda, 106
Alhambra HS
Alhambra

Hubbs, Linda, 65
Lone Pine HS
Lone Pine

Huggins, Vicki Warner,
23, 69, 129
Placer HS
Auburn

Humphry, Marie, 18, 77
Grant Mid. School
Escondido

Hunyadi, Nancy, 18, 34
Fullerton HS
Fullerton

III

Ikkanda, Reiko, 46, 131
South Pasadena HS
South Pasadena

Irvine, Joan, 75
Upland HS
Upland

JJJ

Jackson, Carole, 51
Apple Valley HS
Apple Valley

Jackson, Jennifer, 47
Corning HS
Corning

Jensen, Gwenn, 32
Mira Mesa HS
San Diego

Jones, Dotti, 60
Etiwanda HS
Etiwanda

Jones, Patricia N.,
43, 45, 46, 55, 125
Norwalk HS
Norwalk

Jordan, Nancy, 67
Merced HS
Merced

KKK

Kaylor, Phyllis, 19, 123
Ray A. Kroc Mid. School
San Diego

Kensinger, Connie, 11
El Camino JHS
Santa Maria

Kerby, Norma, 108
Mt. Carmel HS
San Diego

Kleven, Sharon, 7, 15
San Gabriel, HS
San Gabriel

Kramer, Rita, 14
Montebello HS
Montebello

LLL

Landin, Bonnie, 68, 110
Garden Grove HS
Garden Grove

Lee, Donna, 50
Elsinore JHS
Lake Elsinore

Lefler, Susan, 75, 104
Ramona JHS
Chino

Lindrum, Yvonne, 9, 133
Schurr HS
Montebello

Lingenfelter, Susan, 132
Edgewood HS
West Covina

Lopez, Karen, 76
San Luis Obispo HS
San Luis Obispo

Onderko, Mary, 121
Del Campo HS
Fair Oaks

Orr, Myrna, 13, 131
McFadden Int. School
Santa Ana

Osborne, Tess, 6
Columbus-Tustin Int.
Tustin

Owen, Laurie, 2
Hoover HS
San Diego

PPP

Parks, Bonnie, 50
Big Pine HS
Big Pine

Paul, Nan, 9, 81, 93
Grant Mid. School
Escondido

Peck, Pat, 119
Cordova HS
Rancho Cordova

Pepper, Lorraine S., 36
Oceanside HS
Oceanside

Phillips, Merlina, 57, 120
McCloud HS
McCloud

Pierre, Jan, 120
Cabrillo HS
Lompoc

Pius, Bonnie, 63
Sanger HS
Sanger

Priestley, Roberta, 125
Alhambra HS
Alhambra

Pullan, Cheryl, 104, 116
Terrace Hills JHS
Grand Terrace

Putnam, Penny, 2
Divisadero JHS
Visalia

RRR

Raven, Ginger, 110
Chico JHS
Chico

Rayl, Charla, 32
El Toro HS
El Toro

Reaser, Wilma, 70
Hemet JHS
Hemet

Reed, Pam, 12
Redondo Union HS
Redondo Beach

Reed, Vera K. 102
Hesperia JHS
Hesperia

Richmond, Mary E. 11, 18, 27
San Luis Obispo
San Luis Opispo

Riediger, Martha, 109
Sequoia JHS
Simi Valley

Robertson, Lynn, 66, 93
Esparto HS
Esparto

Robinson, Dana, 94
South Mid. School
Downey

Robinson, Linda, 27, 38
Sinaloa JHS
Simi Valley

TTT

Tam, Marilyn, 26
Orange Glen HS
Escondido

Tavaglione, Amy, 45
Etiwanda HS
Etiwanda

Taylor, Deanna, 25, 107
Mesa Verde HS
Citrus Heights

Taylor, Gennan, 74
Bonita HS
La Verne

Taylor, Vicki, 12
Silver Valley HS
Yermo

Thweatt, Marty, 87
Monte Vista HS
Spring Valley

Tice, Rebecca Oppen, 74, 102
Dana Hills HS
Dana Point

Tilson, Karen, 115
Nogales HS
La Puente

Tolson, Maureen, 102
Lompoc Valley Mid. School
Lompoc

Traw, Marianne,
3, 14, 47, 103, 108, 114
Ball JHS
Anaheim

Turk, Jolie, 105
Dunsmuir HS
Dunsmuir

Turner, Sharon, 2
El Dorado HS
Placentia

VVV

Van Camp, Nikki, 123
Poly HS
Riverside

Vickrey, Sandy, 106
Winters HS
Winters

WWW

Walker, Gloria, 26, 82
Casa Roble Fundamental HS
Orangevale

Walling, Lou Ann, 22
Meadowbrook Mid. School
Poway

Walls, Millie, 13
El Dorado, HS
Placentia

Walter, Mary, 126
Mt. Carmel HS
San Diego

Waterbury, Sue, 112
San Luis Obispo HS
San Luis Obispo

Wells, Betty, 40
Oroville HS
Oroville

Whiteley, Ruth, 50
Roosevelt JHS
Kingsburg

Williams, Kathy, 19, 47, 113
Jurupa JHS
Riverside

Wilson, Dorothy, 34, 38, 43, 129
Dale JHS
Anaheim

Worland, Janet, 15
Silver Valley HS
Yermo

YYY

George Yackey, 13
Santana HS
Santee

Yamamoto, D., 25, 107
Mesa Verde HS
Citrus Heights

Yancey, Lisa, 85
San Clemente HS
San Clemente

Yeakel, Geraldine, E., 107
Perris HS
Perris

Yergat, Lou Helen, 65
Mission Viejo HS
Mission Viejo

Yeutter, Carolyn, 15, 21
Norco HS
Norco

ZZZ

Zallar, Sue, 89
Capistrano Valley HS
Mission Viejo

Notes

California's Favorite Mexican Foods
California Cookbook Company
30790 San Pasqual Road
Rancho California, California 92390

Please send _____ copy(ies) of your cookbook at $8.95 each (includes tax and postage). Make checks payable to: *California Cookbook Company.*

Enclosed is my check for $_____.

Name _____

Street _____

City_____State_____Zip_____

California's Favorite Mexican Foods
California Cookbook Company
30790 San Pasqual Road
Rancho California, California 92390

Please send _____ copy(ies) of your cookbook at $8.95 each (includes tax and postage). Make checks payable to: *California Cookbook Company.*

Enclosed is my check for $_____.

Name _____

Street _____

City_____State_____Zip_____

California's Favorite Mexican Foods
California Cookbook Company
30790 San Pasqual Road
Rancho California, California 92390

Please send _____ copy(ies) of your cookbook at $8.95 each (includes tax and postage). Make checks payable to: *California Cookbook Company.*

Enclosed is my check for $_____.

Name _____

Street _____

City_____State_____Zip_____